Frederick Palmer

In the Klondyke

Including an account of a winter's journey to Dawson

Frederick Palmer

In the Klondyke
Including an account of a winter's journey to Dawson

ISBN/EAN: 9783744743297

Printed in Europe, USA, Canada, Australia, Japan

Cover: Foto ©Andreas Hilbeck / pixelio.de

More available books at **www.hansebooks.com**

The Chilkoot Pass.

IN THE KLONDYKE

INCLUDING AN ACCOUNT OF

A WINTER'S JOURNEY TO DAWSON

BY

FREDERICK PALMER

ILLUSTRATED

CHARLES SCRIBNER'S SONS
NEW YORK 1899

TROW DIRECTORY
PRINTING AND BOOKBINDING COMPANY
NEW YORK

CONTENTS

I. THE START FROM DYEA

Choosing Comrades—Jack Beltz and his Dogs—Fritz Gamble—From Sheep Camp to the Summit—Packing over the Chilkoot Pass—The Halt at Lake Linderman—A Night in a Sleeping Bag—Coasting down the Frozen Yukon—Half Way to Dawson . . *Page 1*

II. ON THE TRAIL

Personalities—The Forebears of Jack and Fritz—Good Camp Manners—Dog Individuality—Dude—The Team of Huskies—Wayfarers at Five Fingers—Fort Selkirk and Pelly—The Thanksgiving Turkey that Did Not Get to Dawson—A Diet of Flapjacks—Suburbs of the Klondyke Capital—The Passing of the Trail . *Page 36*

III. DAWSON

Social Aspects of Dawson—Cornering the Tinned Food Market—Cheechawkos and Old-Timers in the Early Days . . *Page 61*

IV. THE FIRST DISCOVERIES

The Beginning of Mining in Alaska—Forty Mile Creek—Canadian and American Deposits—The Largest Log-Cabin Town in the World—Life of the First Adventurers—The Superfluity of Six-Shooters—Leaving the Latch-Strings Out—The Way of the Transgressors—Indian Charley and his Nugget . . . *Page 66*

CONTENTS

V. MINERS AND MINING

Reaping the Gold Harvest—Thawing and Sluicing—Miners and their Theories—The Dome—Expensive Timber—Empty Pockets but Dollars in the Dumps—The First Millionnaires—Color in the Pan—Once a Prospector Always a Prospector—Figuring Fortunes—Capitalists in Demand—The Forty Happy Kings on Eldorado . . . . *Page 85*

VI. SOME KLONDYKE TYPES

The Fool and his Lucky Friends—More Theorizers—Joe Staley and Billy Deddering—French Gulch Bench—Good Fortune that was Deserved—Neighbors and Twins—No Cure for the Gold Fever . . . . *Page 111*

VII. GETTING ACQUAINTED

Mr. and Mrs. "Meenach" and their Menage—The Juvenile Mining Company, Limited—Voss—The Arch-Deacon—A Sour-Dough Stiff—A Dalmatian and a Turk—Siawash George and his Steam-Engine—Miss Mulrooney at The Forks—The Price of a "Square" with Trimmings . . . . *Page 126*

VIII. ARCTIC TRAITS

Daily Life in Dawson—Renting a Cabin—Circumventing the Huskies—Joey Boureau and his Restaurant—The Faro Dealer's Wife and her Bakery—The Laundryman and his Claim—Jack Beltz's Schemes—A Pair of Dreamers . . . . *Page 153*

CONTENTS

IX. PILGRIMS' TRAILS AND TRIALS

Itineraries—Alleged Unimportance of Experience—The Case of Father Stanley—Press Agents and Primers of Wealth—The Secretary of the Seattle Chamber of Commerce his own Convert—Pardners and Promoters—Outfits—Home Comforts for an Arctic Climate—Heterogeneous Boat Loads—The Nancy G—Tragedies of the Passes . . . . *Page 163*

X. PROFITS AND LOSSES

Newspapers as Profit-Winners—Hearing about Dewey—A Drop in Eggs—Market Items—Lemons against Scurvy—The Mercury at 110 Degrees—An Averted Moving Day—Industrious Scavengers—The Klondyke Itself—Aspects of Summer—Bandanna Hats and Pink Lemonade—A Restaurant Trust—The Grasshoppers and the Ants—Disillusions . . . . *Page 181*

XI. GOVERNMENT

The Canadian Policy in the Yukon Province—Taxes and Fees—The Gold Commissioner's Office—Conflicts between Territorial and Dominion Governments—Timber Grants—The Value of the Mounted Police—The Newly Rich at Dawson—The Order of the Yukon Pioneers—Mrs. Constantine . . . . . . *Page 200*

XII. DOWN THE YUKON AND HOME

Good-By to Dawson—The Extinction of the Unfit—Steamboating to St. Michaels—Mosquitoes and Sandbars—Pilgrims by the All-Water Route—Behring Sea—Civilization Once More . *Page 212*

LIST OF ILLUSTRATIONS

The Chilkoot Pass . . . . *Frontispiece*

FACING PAGE

"Packing" Timber 8

Pilgrims Resting on the Chilkoot 8

A Halt 14

Guiding the Team 18

Borrowing a Hint from Ice-Boats—Just Above White Horse Rapids 22

Over the Bench Ice of Thirty Mile River 26

Crossing a Brook 32

In Camp—The Dogs' Porridge 40

The First Boats 54

A Typical Pilgrims' Boat 66

Yukon Indians 78

On the Creeks 88

A Flume on Bonanza Creek 102

Cleaning Up 108

Shovelling a Clean-Up into a Gold Pan 108

The Discoverers of French Gulch Bench at Work . . 124

LIST OF ILLUSTRATIONS

	FACING PAGE
Pardners and Twins for Forty Years	124
Miss Mulrooney of The Forks	142
Jack Beltz	156
"The Huskies"	156
On the Pass	164
Caches of Pilgrims' Outfits at the Summit	172
Bargaining for a Newly Arrived Boat-Load, Dawson	182
In the Camps of the Cheechawkos	188
A Yukon Steamer	198
The Main Street of Dawson	208
A Dawson Good-By	214

IN THE KLONDYKE

IN THE KLONDYKE

I

THE START FROM DYEA

CHOOSING COMRADES—JACK BELTZ AND HIS DOGS—FRITZ GAMBLE—FROM SHEEP CAMP TO THE SUMMIT—PACKING OVER THE CHILKOOT PASS—THE HALT AT LAKE LINDERMAN—A NIGHT IN A SLEEPING BAG—COASTING DOWN THE FROZEN YUKON—HALF WAY TO DAWSON.

ORIGINALLY, I had intended to accompany our Government expedition for the relief of the miners of the Klondyke, which was in part mobilized at Dyea when I arrived there late in February. As it never went any farther, for the good reason that Dawson had been rescued from famine by the migration of a portion of its population, I was left to my own resources. Wholesome fatigue and clean camps on the snow were better than the hospitality of a mushroom town built of rough boards and tar-paper; a little adventure was better than watching for two months the thousands of pilgrims of fortune in the desperate and monotonous labor of putting their outfits over the passes; and I determined, rather than to wait with them for the opening of navigation, to undertake with dogs and sleds of my own the untried journey of six hundred miles over the ice-fields of the Lewes lakes and the ice-packs of the Yukon River which the Government expedition had contemplated.

Whoever was to go with me must be companionable, industrious, and loyal, lest in pitching a tent in a storm, when limbs ached from the strain of the day's tramp, an unruly temper might lead to the crisis of blows or separation. In turn, I must work as hard as he; for we could not afford to carry food for a stomach that nourished idle hands.

Precisely the right kind of comrade, equipped with experience, I had hoped would be forthcoming from among the men who had violated the traditions of the early communities of gold-seekers in regard to winter travel. Some members of this hardy little army were almost daily arriving in Dyea. But their dogs were worn out, and they themselves were inclined to laugh at my suggestion, more particularly at my money. Having pointed out the greater

THE START FROM DYEA

difficulties of ingress than of egress, they asked, with a touch of sarcasm, if I thought that they had made the journey out from Dawson for the purpose of immediately retracing their steps.

Meanwhile, adventurous spirits but lately arrived from Seattle or San Francisco came to offer their services with all the self-confidence characteristic of a floating population. The references of some were belied by their demeanor, and the demeanor of others by their references. All were further belied by their dogs—Newfoundlands, setters, and what not—which had received a few days' training for market purposes in Seattle. In consequence, I was almost despairing, when I was accosted by a powerfully built, blond-haired, blue-eyed fellow who impressed his personality upon me at once.

"I hear you're lookin' for a dog-puncher," he said, awkwardly. "My name's Jack Beltz. I've been a cowboy, and done a good many other things in the West, and now I'm up against it with the crowd in Alaska. I think I could do what you want"—and then with sudden fervor, "but come around and look at the dogs! If the dogs are no good, you don't want me, that's sure."

"Any further references?"

"Well," after a moment's thought, "there's Bangs, up at the Miner's Rest. He knowed me when I was on a ranch in Nebrasky. Dunno what he'll say. You can ask him, though. Anyhow, I'd be obliged if you'd see the dogs 'fore you make a decision."

He waited outside the Miner's Rest while I spoke with Bangs.

"Jack Beltz!" exclaimed Bangs. "Well, Jack Beltz's a fool when it comes to hosses and dawgs. He thinks they can talk. But Jack Beltz'll stick to a thing that's hard—he don't like things that ain't—till he comes out of it or goes down with it, and all the mules in the army couldn't make him mad."

Then I followed Jack to a woodpile in the outskirts of the town, where five fat and sleek huskies awoke at his approach, and at his command lined up like so many soldiers, wagging their bushy tails over their backs and watching his every movement with their sharp eyes. From their mothers, who were native Indian dogs, they had inherited their affection for man, however poor the specimen, and from their fathers, who were full-blooded wolves of the forest, their strength and endurance.

THE START FROM DYEA

In an hour after I had met him I had engaged Jack Beltz on the strength of the fat on his dogs' ribs, of his blue eyes, and of Bangs's candid recommendation. Placing my theoretical knowledge of the needs of an arctic climate against his experience as a frontiersman, we quickly made out a list of the supplies which were to be packed on our sleds, minimizing everything in weight and bulk as far as we dared, but being very careful to consider that while we might go hungry the dogs must not. In all, we took eleven hundred pounds, four hundred of food and bedding for ourselves and seven hundred of food for the dogs.

Chance made the choice of a third member of the party, whose assistance was necessary, as happy as the choice of its second. This big fellow, over six feet in height, was Frederick Gamble, known to his friends as Fritz, who had given up a career as an artist and had already spent one unprofitable season with a pick and a pack in the Cassiar district. No pilgrim accustomed to good living ever accepted a diet of bacon and beans with better philosophy.

It was already the 18th of March. If, as the old-timers said, the Yukon became impassable by the 20th of April, we had little time to spare. There was much in our surroundings on the day of our departure to lend credence to their opinion. The sun, at midday, which turned the blue of the little glaciers over our heads into a red, united with the wind blowing from the ocean to thaw the snow on the mountain sides. In the many places where the winter trail had been worn down to the sand of the flats which the Dyea River overflows in the freshets of spring, the pilgrims had to turn off to the still intact but spongy ice of the winding little stream of the autumn and winter to find a better track for their sleds.

Canyon City, where the comparatively level stretch of eight miles of the flats is at an end and the real ascent of eight miles to the summit of the Pass begins, had grown into a little village with three saloons since I had last visited it, only two weeks before. Here the river is a thundering cataract in spring, dashing through a narrow gorge of rocks which rise to a height of from twenty to a hundred feet. The sled road of trodden snow with a basis of ice had become so mushy that the men who panted forward, dragging their sleds and asking with their eyes, if not with their tongues, for

THE START FROM DYEA

a hand to help them out of ruts, were wondering whether they would not be forced to take to the summer trail running over the wall of the canyon on the morrow.

Beyond the canyon was a community of thousands of tents, Sheeps Camp, a halfway station in the work of transportation from Dyea to the Summit if not in the number of miles. It had doubled if not trebled in population since I had last seen it, which meant that the bulk of the pilgrims had their outfits this far on their journey. I slept here, the guest of some friends who had an excellent bed of fir boughs. Before I was up I knew that the day on the Summit was fair by the tramping of the packers and the howls of the dogs in the main path, or street, of the "town." At this time, most of the days on the Summit were fair, and it behooved the pilgrims to make the most of them. In midwinter it often happened that intense cold and a fierce storm of fine snow, resembling a blizzard in the Dakotas, made the Summit impassable.

The series of steep ascents leading from Sheep Camp to the base of the final, long, and much steeper ascent, called as a whole by the pilgrims the Summit, was a struggling line of men and dogs, drawing sleds, and of horses with packs. Oaths and howls were so numerous that no one oath or howl came to the ear distinctly. You heard only noise, as you hear an uproar of individual shouts at a national convention. In the early days the pioneers had given to the little plateau at the base of the final ascent the name of the Scales, because at this point they were wont to balance their packs and readjust them for the last grim effort. Beyond this neither horse nor mule could carry nor dog could draw a load. The more supple animal man took his place.

If you would see the Pass, of which so much was written when so little was known of the Klondyke itself, you have only to imagine a broad incline at an angle of nearly forty-five degrees, seven hundred feet in height, running between two snowy peaks at its summit, with men in the foreground bending under the weight of heavy packs, and gradually growing smaller as they ascend, until, finally, they seem like ants dangerously near toppling over with their loads, though, to your relief and amazement, crawling off the white blanket into the sky.

Pilgrims Resting on the Chilkoot.

"Packing" Timber.

THE START FROM DYEA

In the hard, well-packed snow, steps had been cut, making it a case of walking upstairs rather than of climbing. At intervals, more welcome than the chairs on the landings of an apartment house which has no elevator, seats had been cut. Men stepping out of the slow-moving line found rest in these. It was not "game" to groan, but purple faces and lungs gasping for more power for bodies quivering with excess of strain told of misery that was felt if not expressed. When a man did break down he collapsed utterly, and sometimes he wept.

Fifty pounds was the usual weight of a pack for all who did not take pride in exhibiting their brute strength. These, and the professional packers who bore the outfits of pilgrims who could afford this luxury, often labored under a hundred pounds or more. The hero of the day was an Indian. He took up a barrel weighing three hundred and fifty pounds. A Swede who crawled up on his hands and knees with three six-by-four timbers strapped on his back shared honors with him, however. The descent to the Scales was delightfully simple. You sat down and tobogganed, using your heels as a brake, without any unpleasant results if you had well-riveted overalls.

On the crest were piled hundreds of pilgrims' outfits, separated one from another by narrow paths, making the whole seem like a city in miniature. Buried under the seventy feet of snow which had fallen during the winter were two other such cities, which their owners hoped to recover in the summer. Beyond floated a large British flag over the little block-house where the British Northwest Mounted Police had established themselves to collect customs and to see that no one not having a special permit entered Canadian territory with less than a year's supply of food.

Jack labored for two hours in bringing up the dogs with the empty sleds, while our goods came on the backs of the ants, who charged three cents a pound for the service. Aside from the five huskies hitched to a large basket-sled, we had two St. Bernards, "Patsy" and "Tim," who were born in the country, and duly christened and acclimatized there. With "Patsy" and "Tim," and my hand on the "gee-pole" by which the sled was guided, I went under fire for the first time in descending the inland side of the pass. Man and sled were put *hors de combat* again and again, while the dogs, who managed to keep erect, looked back on me with professional disgust. I wanted to blame my misfortunes to my moccasins, but Jack wore moccasins as well and maintained his footing easily. Fortunately for the novice there are three small lakes—at the time they were three fields of snow—in the nine miles from the Summit to Linderman, and he could take advantage of the respite when he was trotting across these to think out, in the hard-and-fast civilized manner, how to avoid his frequent loss of equilibrium.

We spent the night "at home" with Jack in his own camp on the shore of Lake Linderman. Jack and his "pardner" Cliff had been among the pilgrims who had attempted to reach Dawson in the same summer that the news of the great "strike" was received by the outside world. The ice formed in the lakes and rivers before they could build their boats, and there had been nothing to do but to wait eight months until the ice was gone. Once he had bought a team of dogs, however, Jack became enamoured of making the journey now at last before him. On the other hand nothing apparently had disturbed the patience of Cliff, who was a broad-shouldered giant, over six feet in height. The pair had first met in Seattle, formed an alliance "for dust or bust," as Cliff said, and had thought more of each other "every minute ever since." Cliff was to stay at Linderman now, but their alliance was resumed later in Dawson, when Jack, Fritz, and I dissolved partnership.

While we were putting our outfits straight and Jack was writing a letter—from his sighs I concluded that it was to his best girl—Cliff cooked flapjacks and fried bacon, sang snatches of what had been the latest popular songs when he left Colorado, and talked to his favorite dog, a Great Dane, who was as scarred as a veteran.

"Think you're going to be slighted, don't you, Maje?" he rambled on. "Froze off your ears already, ain't you? 'Tain't no country for short-haired dogs, is it? Don't want to lose your tail, too. No, sir. You're going to sleep in the tent same's ever, and if they don't like it I'll tell you 'sickum,' and they won't be with us long."

Major curled up at Cliff's feet as usual that night. Inasmuch as he had a snow-bath whenever he was caught in a storm, he was more

THE START FROM DYEA

agreeable than many human beings whose bodies had not touched water for months.

In a day we had passed over the only portion of our journey on land, and we were henceforth, as Jack put it gayly, to proceed downhill with the current of the river at the rate of eight inches to the mile, which is fast enough as currents go, but rather poor coasting. The course of the Yukon through the heart of Alaska is in a semicircle, with one end at the coast and the other end as near to the coast as the head-waters of a stream can be, unless it flows on the level. Once he has reached the lakes, the prospector may float for 2,600 miles to Bering Sea, and but for this one of the two friendly deeds of nature in Alaska—the other is abundant firewood—it is questionable if the gold in the Klondyke would have been discovered in our generation. De Soto's exploring party would have had a similar advantage if the Mississippi had risen within thirty-two miles of Cape Hatteras, and they would have needed it if the valley of the Mississippi had been like the valley of the Yukon.

In harnessing our dogs at dawn, as we looked out across Lake Linderman from Jack's camp, the only color in sight in the vast expanse of white was the needle-like fir-trees, cropping through the snow on the mountain-sides, and the outlines of a few pilgrims in advance of the main body, already astir, dragging their sleds on to Lake Bennett, where, with whipsaws, hammers, nails, oakum, and pitch, was to be built out of the forests the unique and variegated flotilla which was to line the river-banks in front of Dawson in May and June. Jack snapped the long lash of his whip, shook the "gee-pole" to free the runners, cried "Mush!"—a Saxon contraction of the "*Marchons!*" brought into the country along with many other words by the French Canadians—and seven gallant four-footed comrades and three figures in parkees looking like hooded night-shirts began in earnest their journey over the trail hardened by the pilgrims' footsteps. By the wayside we passed caches of waterproof bags, one of them at either end of a pilgrim's route of daily toil in moving his outfit forward by relays, his own ambition making him undergo longer hours and greater strain than he, a free citizen (U. S. A.), would have endured for any other master.

Linderman is only four miles long, and we

were soon on Bennett, where the afternoon brought, in sharp contrast to the keen atmosphere of the morning, a blowing storm of moist snow which wet us to the skin. When Jack halted the dogs for our first and our worst camp, whose only consolation was a water-hole that had been made by some pilgrim, they set up a howl of knowing delight.

With the snow up to my waist I cut firewood out of the abundance of dead timber, and then cut green spruce-boughs, which, when laid tufts upward on the snow that was packed down as a floor for our seven-by-seven tent, made a soft bed. Then I went for a pail of water and brought in my sleeping-bag, and my work was done. The air had cleared suddenly, and the weather had turned so cold that my parkee had frozen as stiff as a board. I pulled it off, substituted dry moccasins and socks for my wet ones, left the rest of my clothes to be dried by the warmth of my body, and then, huddling myself up with my sleeping-bag as a seat, I watched my comrades finishing their allotted tasks.

Fritz, who had been chosen cook, was sitting with one leg on either side of the little sheet-iron stove, smoking a cigarette and making flapjacks. Outside, by the light of the crackling blaze, I could see Jack stirring something in a pan over a roaring fire with a big ladle that he had whittled out of a sapling. Weirdly presiding over this operation, their bodies in shadow and their wolf-noses thrust forward with epicurean relish, were the huskies. Jack fed them only once a day, but then all that they could eat of tallow, bacon, cornmeal, and rice, thoroughly boiled in the form of a porridge. When he took the pan off the fire he put it, safely covered, in the snow to cool, while the dogs mounted guard over it, glaring at one another; and then he came to sit on his own bed, and together we ate by the light of a candle hanging by a piece of wire from the top of the tent. As I had my granite-ware plate filled with beans the second time and took my fourth flapjack—a flapjack an inch thick and seven inches in diameter—a twinkle came into Jack's eyes.

"I like to see a man in earnest," he said.

Then he relighted his pipe and went back to his dogs. Having filled a two-quart tin pan for each of them, with the ardor of a child he heaped more timber on the dying fire, and, turning his back to the cheerful glow, began a technical conversation on the state of the trail with sleek old Dude, the leader of the team.

Later, when he returned to the tent, the dogs were so many balls of fur, their noses snuggled under their bushy tails. If two feet of snow had fallen during the night it would not have disturbed the serenity of their slumbers, and in the morning at the call to harness they would have dug their way out and shaken themselves ready for duty. Jack explained, as he pulled off his moccasins, that they had eaten only half their usual rations. Having been treated to beefsteak in Dyea by their generous owner, they rather resented marching fare; but they would come down to it as soon as they felt the pangs of hunger, he added.

"Are you tired?" I asked him.

"Me? No," he drawled.

He filled up the stove—he must always have a fire of some kind going—and, leaning back on his robe, his hands behind his head, he looked up at the top of the tent dreamily. He was still in this attitude when I crawled into my sleeping-bag and quickly fell asleep. The sleeping-bag did well enough for that night, but I soon repented of it. With no opportunity for airing it properly, it soon collected moisture and became as a uncomfortable as a coating of ice. After I had been kept awake for a night by the colder weather that followed the storm, I ripped it open and used the furs as a robe, which, with the assistance of a heavy blanket, kept me as warm as toast, though, when I awoke, there was a glacial path through the space I had left open for breathing. The wonder to me was that Jack did not freeze his nose—it was a large nose—for he always slept with his head completely outside of his coverings, his beard becoming as white with ice as that of Father Christmas.

"Blister me if I want to smother!" was his explanation.

The first one to awake in the morning crawled half-way out of his robe, and, dexterously leaning over, put the coffee-pot on the stove and made the fire out of the kindlings which were always ready. To dress was to put on your footwear, which had been drying—if it had not been burning—before the stove. Then the robes and blankets were rolled up and strapped to serve as seats for breakfast, and you stepped outside into the invigorating air and did what you might in the way of cleanliness. For my part, I washed my hands in the snow,

Guiding the Team.

using soap liberally, with astonishingly efficacious results. After breakfast we had to pack all the things that we had unpacked the night before back on the sleds and lash them.

On the Lewes lakes, and the streams which join them in a chain, one day was quite like another, with the exception of a single event of importance to ourselves. At daybreak we were on the level trail, now trotting and then walking, until our stomachs cried a halt. On three occasions we had luncheon in the tents of pilgrims who, not having been able to bring their supplies over the pass in the rush of the previous autumn before winter was at hand, were making for the foot of Lake Le Barge to take advantage of the three weeks by which the clearing of the ice in the river precedes the clearing of the ice in the lakes. While his partner was dragging his sled, one of our hosts was suffering in his tent the torture of snow-blindness as the penalty of having gone for a day without glasses. Another host, an old Dane from San Francisco, had no companion, not even a dog.

"Sometime I do get mad," he said, "when the sled pull so hard, and I say, 'Yohn, you are a big fool to start for Klondyke when you are sixty-nine.' But we do not like to gif up. Nefer do we get so old we tank it too late to make a fortune. If a man know as he would drop dead on top of the Pass, I tank a man go on to see the t'ing out. I make a fortune t'ree time, and efery time I haf many pad lucks —yes, very many pad lucks. Sometime I get lonely, and then I say, 'Yohn, there is your wife, there is your shildren; it is Sunday dinner, and you are home with a pile of gold.'"

How we relished the one rapidly diminishing ham that we had brought with us for our first luncheons, followed by the perfect relaxation which comes with good digestion and physical fatigue, glorified by a pipe, before we arose and turned our steps toward the brown line of sled-track which stretched out over the expanse of white until growing darkness made it dim, and Jack began to look out for the first favorable place for a camp!

At this time it was reported that a great "strike" of $2.50 to the pan had been made on Walsh Creek, a tributary of the Yukon near Big Salmon. The rumor afterwards turned out to be an exaggeration—only thirty cents a pan being the amount actually found, which had grown as it travelled up the lakes.

THE START FROM DYEA

Many of the pilgrims, among them ourselves, who already had their year's supply of food over the Pass, and some who had not but were able to elude the police, leaving their caches in charge of friends, put a tent, half a side of bacon, a few quarts of flour, and a few quarts of beans on a sled behind a lean house-dog, and hastened toward Walsh Creek without regard to fatigue or exposure. A sallow and swarthy Quixote who had not made even this provision for his stomach and none for his back except a small blanket, called upon us one morning when we were at breakfast. Before he asked for something to eat he introduced himself as a Cuban who had been a cook in New York, but had concluded to be a cook no more now that fortunes were to be had for a little hard travelling.

"You see, gents," he further explained, assuming a serene air of fellowship, "I've been walking at night so's to get past the police stations. They won't let a feller by when he ain't got any grub. If I carried grub I'd be too late for the strike, mebbe."

"But you'll observe, I'm thinkin'," Jack suggested, "that hotels are few and far between in this region."

"Oh, I'll manage to get on somehow. There's a lot of luck in this world if you dodge about so it'll hit you. I didn't know where I'd get my breakfast, but I've got it, that's sure."

He wished us much happiness, put his blanket on his back, and walked on as unconcernedly as if he had a whole baggage train at his heels. But this was not until he had suggested with the aplomb of the Bowery that we would do well to take him on as a "pardner." What became of him I do not know. Possibly his body lies among a pile of driftwood on some sandbar in the river. On the other hand, I should not be surprised to see him one day on Broadway, a huge diamond in his shirt bosom and a blond lady on his arm, or to read an account of him in a newspaper under the head of "From Cook to Millionaire."

The Walsh Creek digression caused two weeks' delay at a time when we felt the need of every day to complete our journey, and I accept the awkward responsibility for it. At White Horse Canyon we were offered the hospitality of a large cabin with a kitchen in one end and bunk-room in the other, occupied

Borrowing a Hint from Ice-Boats—Just Above White Horse Rapids.

by some workmen engaged in building a tramway around the rapids. Jack suggested that we stop here for a day because the dogs needed rest, he said, but really on my account, I think. I had contracted a bad cough, and my legs ached like two great teeth. In the afternoon I lay down on the cook's bunk, and toward evening Fritz started down the trail to a distant camp to find a doctor who had turned pilgrim of fortune. Meanwhile Jake, the cook, dosed me with tea made of sage that he had gathered on the mountain-side.

"Your pulse is up to a hundred and ten," the doctor said; "but all that you've got is a plain, old-fashioned case of measles. You must have caught them in Dyea, and you've greatly exaggerated them by physical strain."

My comrades put up a tent in another cabin which still wanted doors and windows, thus ensuring a soft light for the protection of my eyes, which the doctor feared might be affected. They nailed some saplings together for a bedstead, and were so ingenious in many ways, so kind in keeping the temperature the same night and day, and in attending to my wants generally, that I felt like a king in his private hospital. Jake came in every day to make sure that I was taking the doses of sage-tea that he sent in morning, noon, and night; while the big workmen came in to hint that I must not let Jake have his own way too much. And I lay on my back and thought of two things—strawberries and pineapples. I would have given all my wealth for either—but not a five-cent piece for a pear.

My convalescence was not so dull as I sat on a bench in the kitchen, learning, under Jake's tutelage, how to cook oatmeal properly, how to bake bread and to make good pies out of dried apples, and listening to him expound his ideas of the world. He was a great cynic. If you believed in one thing, he was sure to believe in another. One of his favorite remarks with which he baited me was that "everybody is out for the stuff; there ain't no honor nowadays; and you don't catch me missin' no dollars." His boarders excused him by saying, "Any cook that's been in a minin'-camp or a lumber-camp is always a blisterin' crank." On the morning of my departure I held out a bill to Jake in partial remuneration for what he had done for me. He stirred the contents of his pot this way and that, viciously, without replying. I protested, and then he growled:

' Gwan! What d'ye take me for?"

As I waved him a good-by he called out:

"Young feller, you're all right, but you won't argue."

In two days we were at the foot of Lake Le Barge, and on the second of these we had travelled thirty-five miles, which made the dogs very unfit for service on the day following.

So all of another two days' hard work was required to go from the foot of Le Barge to the junction of the Hootalinqua over a portion of the Yukon known from its length as Thirty Mile River, and certainly worthy of some distinction on account of other characteristics. Many more boats of the pilgrims' flotilla were wrecked in the spring on its hidden rocks than in the White Horse Rapids, which, I may add, have received undue celebrity. If an average temperature of thirty degrees below zero continues for several weeks, the current may freeze over, but rarely is there more than bench ice along the shores; and this, owing to the increasingly moderate weather and the falling water, was fast breaking away in huge cakes, which fell into the stream with a splash. Over that which remained, slippery, sometimes sloping toward the river at a considerable angle, and often only a foot or two in breadth, we must make our way. When there was no footing below the sled, we attached one end of a rope to it, wrapped the other end around our waists, and if one of us slipped and fell in the soft snow of the steep hill-side above, luckily the others maintained their hold and were able to prevent both sleds and dogs from going into the river and putting an end to our little expedition there and then.

There was only one accident, and that not alarming. Fritz thought that he did not need our help to bring the St. Bernards over a place that the big sled had safely crossed with Jack's back and mine against it and with the heavy steel prongs strapped to the heels of our boots dug into the ice. We heard a cry of " Hurry up ! This is cold !" and looked around to see Fritz standing in a shallow eddy up to his waist, his parkee blown up about his head like a veritable balloon, while he braced himself against the sled. "I had to jump in to save our bedding," he said. We hurried on the faster so that he might keep his blood in circulation, and he merely took the trouble to change his socks when we made a camp on a fairly comfortable ice-cake, after having as-

Over the Bench Ice of Thirty-Mile River.

sured ourselves that it would not float away with us during the night.

Near the Hootalinqua the current slackens, and we crossed where the stream was completely frozen over. Above us was a great jam of cakes that had floated down, some of which rumbled under our feet, came out in an open place below, and then went on to form another jam. A few minutes later there was a boom and our bridge moved downstream with the noise of a medley of bass drums. At noon on this day the sun had made the trail so soft that we sank into it up to our knees. We halted a little later, determined to start at one o'clock in the morning and take advantage of the crust frozen during the night; and we had what seemed at the time the good fortune to put up in a cabin which had been abandoned by the mounted police. Having had an early dinner, we were thinking of bed at six o'clock when two ragged men, their faces blackened by cooking over camp-fires, came in. They sat down, and when they had eaten with the heartiness of famished beings some things that we had left on the table, one of them, whom his companion called "the Doctor," became explanatory:

"You mustn't mind our appetites," he said. We've just come from Dawson. My pardner there, Yukon Bill, hain't been out of the country for eight years. Go easy there, Bill! Your manners are bad."

"Shut up!" roared Bill, looking as wild as a hungry lynx.

"Oh, he ain't as crazy as Jim," continued the Doctor. "Jim was a sight uglier 'n Bill, an' you can see what Bill is. He took his share of the bacon on his back an' started out for himself this mornin'."

"No packin' fer me! We kept the dogs, you bet, by ——," put in Bill through a mouthful.

Jim arrived three hours later. Without paying any attention to the presence of other persons, he dropped his pack as if it were of lead, fell down on the bench, pushed back his unkempt hair, and looked vacantly at the stove.

"Hello, Jim, you loon!" the Doctor called out. "As long's we've said quits, I ain't goin' to be mean. Have one of our flapjacks!"

"Eat yer own dirt," replied Jim. "I kin cook, an' I've got just as much right in this cabin as you have." And Jim put a skillet with a piece of dirty bacon in it on the stove.

"Don't push my pan off there, you eight-footed elephant!" cried the Doctor.

Jim lifted his skillet and turned on the Doctor. Then he set the skillet down again with the action of one who is too tired for further effort, and fell back onto his seat.

"You Siawash sons of the devil," he said between his teeth, "if I ever git my strength on the outside I'll lick both on ye till ye bawl like a calf." And brushing back his hair again he added, in a protesting voice, after a moment's pause: "I kin do it, too!"

"Bully old Jim!" observed the Doctor.

It was plain enough that the minds of all three of our visitors, especially Jim, had been affected by the hardships that they had endured on their long tramp, with only snow, trees, dogs, and their own quarrels for companionship. Most of these grim travellers whom we met coming out from Dawson—now and then one was limping from scurvy—had neither tent nor stove, quite inadequate robes, no dishes except skillets and cups, and no food except bacon, flour, and beans, and not always beans. Earlier in the winter they put up a barrier of boughs against the wind, and slept between two great fires, kept up by the member of the party whose night it was to watch.

At eleven o'clock the Doctor stopped talking, and we slept for half an hour, only to be awakened by the arrival of another equally worn-out party, and almost the last one from Dawson that we met. By the time we were fairly asleep again these tired beings set the cabin on fire, and Jack, in his good-natured way, put the flames out for them.

At daylight I was awakened by Fritz, who was grumbling to himself about the audacity and the stomachs that some people must have. I arose to see him looking into two empty pails which he had left full of apple-sauce and beans.

"I was hungry as a dog in the night," the Doctor explained, a little later, "and I couldn't help it."

Fritz replied by looking daggers at him. Then the Doctor offered a pair of snow-shoes to Fritz as an olive branch.

"If I thought that what you've eaten would make you downright sick, I'd take 'em," said Fritz.

"'Twon't," replied the Doctor, in all honesty. "Nothin' makes me sick." And he gave the

THE START FROM DYEA

snow-shoes to Jack, whose eyes were twinkling in appreciation of the conversation.

As we started out, five or six hours later than we had planned, we resolved to eschew cabins hereafter. We had not done a half-day's work when a heavy wet snow set in, and the condition of the dogs compelled us to rest.

"Wear 'em out," said Jack, "and it's all up, anyway. We'll boil some beans and lay up some sleep ahead against a freeze."

Accordingly, dogs and men slept for thirteen hours.

So slight was the freeze at night that the sun, now rising at four o'clock, soon thawed the crust. The Big Salmon was already open, its current destroying the trail and leaving a field of slush with many places too deep for passage for a distance of five or six miles, which was as wearing on the dogs as a full day's journey under ordinary circumstances. We only hoped that the Big Salmon was alone in its enmity to our plans, for once the ice is out of the tributaries, the ice in the Yukon cannot last long. It seemed to be imperative that, in order to take full advantage of the slight crust which formed, we should travel nights. We made this experiment once, starting out at 10 P.M., and once was quite enough.

The thawing snow had fallen away from the path, which was hardened by travel from Dawson and therefore the better resisted the sun's rays; but when frozen it was as slippery as ice. In so far as you were able to keep the sled from slewing on this razor's back, that much you aided the dogs. At intervals you walked outside the trail, plunging with every step through the crust down to the slush underneath, while, with body bent and arm extended with all the rigidity at your command, you endeavored to hold the lurching "gee-pole" steady. Early in the evening the great darkness seemed the more dense to visions strained by the sun beating on the expanse of snow by day. With their eyes bloodshot and almost closed with snow-blindness, the St. Bernards continually stumbled and fell as they leaped from one side of the trail to the other, blindly and vainly seeking a better footing. When we rested we dug holes in the crust, and throwing ourselves prostrate, drank our fill. At first, I tried to use a telescope drinking-cup, but soon I regarded it as tawdry, inefficient, and unworthy of the occasion, and fol-

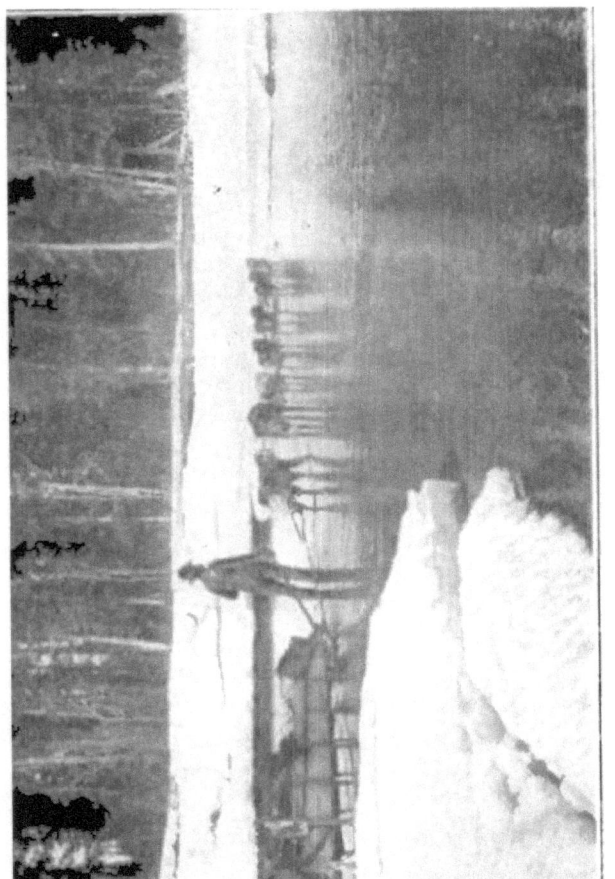

Crossing a Brook.

lowed the more robust custom of Jack, who enjoyed to the full the pleasure of having made a convert. For one who had left White Horse with a bad cough on the heels of the measles, such indulgence would seem to be the height of indiscretion. But the cough was completely gone, no room having been left for it in the development of every muscle of my body by the handling of the "gee-pole."

At these times we would pay our respects with some bitterness to the man who had made this strange and lonely trail, though in better moments we were willing to admit that he was a pioneer and a pathfinder. As soon as the ice would bear him, when the wind had drifted the snow here and there and lifted the slush ice up to be frozen into rifts, with his dogs and sleds he set his face toward the coast, winding in and out between these rifts, back and forth across the stream and along its banks, wherever he could find the best footing; and all who came afterward followed in his footsteps. He was making a path for himself and not for us, and it was to his interest, if not to ours, to have it as crooked as the track of a snake, and on the most crooked of rivers at that.

With the falling of the water as the winter advanced, the ice was rent with cracks. It fell away from the shores, leaving cakes on end and fissures. You must toil up one side of a pyramid to slide down the other; you held your sled up literally at an angle of forty-five degrees, and sometimes you dropped up to your hips into the fissures, for the thin covering of snow often made them invisible even in the daytime. Yet to step away from the trail was like stepping off a bad corduroy road into a swamp.

In the darkness the trained eye of the master had to trust to the halt and whine of the brave little Dude when we came to a place where the surface water was deep or the ice had given away entirely. While the master went ahead with a pole to make soundings, Fritz seized the opportunity to roll a cigarette and to say in a drawl, as he sat on his sled, resting:

"If I were in town I would call a cab."

Jack had discarded his boots with sharp pegs —the three of us had worn boots since it became warmer—to put on moccasins. These were soon wet and quickly froze, giving him a sole of ice with which to walk on ice. In utter exhaustion, once the big fellow threw himself upon his "gee-pole" and gasped out something about not caring whether he went any farther or not. Then he added:

"Well, we'll outlast this trail, anyway. I guess I'll light my pipe."

Confessedly, I was rather glad of the incident. It is good to see giants nod when you have nodded yourself. Only on the previous day, over a mile of sidling trail, leaning on my sled to keep it from upsetting, and righting it when it did upset, I had momentarily, I am ashamed to say, turned cynic and protester.

An hour before dawn a scimeter of light shot across the heavens, followed by broadswords, fans, daggers, waves, and streaks of light, dancing sometimes in playful panic and again moving in a sweep of dignity. With the aurora borealis as our candle, we passed around Freeman's Point, built a fire for luncheon in a cove, and enjoyed keenly the fact that we were half way to Dawson.

II

ON THE TRAIL

Personalities—The Forbears of Jack and Fritz—Good Camp Manners — Dog Individuality — Dude — The Team of Huskies—Wayfarers at Five Fingers—Fort Selkirk and Pelly—The Thanksgiving Turkey that Did Not Get to Dawson—A Diet of Flapjacks—Suburbs of the Klondyke Capital—The Passing of the Trail.

AS we moved on slowly at dawn to make a few more miles before camping, we saw the penalty of this savage run, which human stubbornness had insisted upon making, in the blood left on the trail by the wounded feet of our dogs. Jack at once covered them with the moccasins which he had brought for the purpose. It was plain enough that the continuance of night marches was unfeasible if we desired our brave steeds to hold out as far as Dawson. While the sled slid easier at night, the excrescences of ice were as sharp as lances, and though the mushy trail of mid-day made the sled harder to pull, it was like a cushion for a wounded foot. We compromised upon a portion of both evils by determining to start at dawn and travel as fast and as long as we could, practically. This gave only seven or eight hours on the road as against the twelve or more that we had originally planned, and in order to make the most of them we made the sacrifice for the dogs' sake of drinking ice-water for our luncheon instead of taking the time to boil chocolate. Fritz preferring to handle the "gee-pole," and I preferring to assist in keeping the equilibrium of the big sled by holding the handles at the rear, each settled down to this as his definite labor.

We now had more time for our camps; more time for our pipes of relaxation as we sat on our beds around Jack's bonfires after the dogs were fed and dinner was eaten. On one of these nights we were talking of ambitions.

"As a boy, I wanted to drive a street-car," said Fritz. "When I grew older they still called me Freddy, and I made pictures for a living. That is enough to ruin any man; and, foreseeing this, I concluded that I'd live on flapjacks and go unwashed, and be called 'pardner,' or Pete, or Bill, or make baking-powder dough, or anything, till I found a good placer mine.

Then I'm going around the world, smoking the best brand of Turkish cigarettes, and looking at other people's pictures."

Jack had run away from home at the age of thirteen to the land of the Indians that had been revealed to him in a dime novel secreted in a haymow, and had earned his own living ever since. Meagre as was his early education, he had picked up a surprising amount of information from reading and from association. His eye was that of a scout; his knowledge of birds and animals that of a naturalist; his love of flowers that of a sentimentalist. He had varied his life as a cowboy by many other occupations. At one time he had been a private coachman in Omaha, just to see how it would seem.

"I was gettin' pretty sick of the job," he explained, "when the old lady I drove about leaned over to me one day, confidentially. 'I'm goin' to get you a fine livery to wear,' she said. Then I realized how low I had fallen, and that evening I was a free man again."

He was longer on the Government survey than in any other employment, rising until he filled a position of considerable responsibility. Possibly it was then that he learned the ethics of camp-life; more likely they were innate. He adhered to his own soap, his own towel, and his own bedding, and was more observant of the small niceties of life than are most of the men who wear the high collars that he despised. In all of his seventeen years of wandering his greatest source of sorrow was that he had never made enough money, according to his ideas, to return home, though his pay had been as high as a hundred and fifty dollars a month. He must have a few thousands, and treat the little Pennsylvania village that was his birthplace to such extravagance as it had never seen before. If he made a "stake" in the Klondyke, he had planned to drive right up to the old folks' door with his team of huskies and a little red cart, distributing candy to the children as the procession moved forward.

The dogs, which at first seemed to me to be only so many domesticated wolves of like dispositions, had now assumed strong individualities. Dude, the leader, was worthy of the name given to him, on account of his sleek coat of thick gray fur, by the frontiersman who had instilled into him the wisdom of the trail and soldierly spirit and obedience. He was the sergeant-major among Yukon dogs, far from being a pup in years and far from having lost his vigor. When called to harness in the morning he would stretch his body, arch his neck, throw his handsome tail over his back, deliver himself of a peculiar little wolfish whine, and trot straight to his place. Though your old sergeant-major may feel a little stiff when he gets out of bed, he isn't stiff when he has his tunic on, especially if there are any recruits about. From the moment that Jack called "Mush!" until he called "Halt!" Dude pulled steadily. All the others shirked at times and needed the crack of the whip to remind them of their duty, but the traces between Dude and the dog behind him were always taut. He had the natural dignity requisite to his position. The other dogs attempted no familiarities with him, such as eating out of his dish or trying to bowl him over in sport. After an unusually hard day's work, before lying down to rest, he would gambol a little with them as a relaxation from the steady strain in harness, but not in a manner of equality.

During their conversations while the master was stirring the porridge he asked the sergeant-major what he thought of the prospects of reaching Dawson before the ice went out of

In Camp—The Dogs' Porridge.

the river, Dude replied, on the authority of Jack's translation:

"Don't ask me! I can make it all right. But we ain't certain of anything as long as we have those house-dogs on the hind sled."

Next to Dude was Fox, a nondescript, who remained in good flesh up to the last. He waddled and puffed in trying to keep up when Dude trotted. Fritz said that Fox reminded him of a fat school-girl, her cheeks daubed with molasses candy, and two braids down her back.

Behind Fox was Jack, a pup, a mischief-maker, a rascal, and an actor. All husky dogs are thieves. Some will take a pot off a stove by its handle and hide it safely out of sight in the snow while they wait for its contents to cool to their taste. Jack promised to become the most accomplished of the clan. His wolf's nose always told him where our bacon was stored and his wolf's eyes told him when his opportunity had arrived. Once he had the meat out of his own basin of porridge eaten, he looked up to see which dog had any left and got it before the other dog realized what was up. He would scent an Indian camp even before Dude, sometimes at a distance of two miles. In the traces he forgot to pull while he looked at the ravens flying overhead or listened for noises in the forest. Then the whip descended upon him and he would seem very crestfallen for a moment, only to be at his old tricks and to have his tail in the air in the next. The more he was punished for dereliction during the day, the greater was his affection for his master in camp. On the warmer nights when Jack slept outside of the hut for the sake of elbow room, he would put himself on guard at the head of the master's bed of boughs and allow no other dog except Dude to come near.

Dude was partial to him. He regarded Jack as a wayward but clever pup who was sowing his wild oats, and he knew, as an old sergeant-major, that this would make the best kind of a dog in the end. Often the master took hold of the ne'er-do-well's ears and shook him, saying:

"I guess I like you best, after all, Jack. That's the way of the world. You're a rascal, but you're clever."

Next in line was Tommy, Jack's brother. Jack enjoyed getting Tommy into scrapes and then leaving him to get out of them the best he could. Tommy was forever sneaking about the tent, and he was so impolitic in his choice of his moment of action that he was usually caught red-handed and cuffed. Though he never succeeded in stealing half as much as Jack, he came in for a great deal more enmity from Fritz than all the rest of the team. Jack used to approach Fritz gayly as Fritz sat with a leg on either side of our little stove, turn his coyote's head to one side, cock up his ears, and assure Fritz of his friendship for a good cook and his contempt for all such curs as Tommy. He might go and come many times in this way before Fritz's back was turned. When it was, however, he seized his spoil and trotted away in the businesslike manner of a dog who is doing an errand for his master. At a safe distance, he neatly dodged all missiles and smiled mockingly back at the cook. When Tommy was licked in the traces he howled for half an hour and his tail did not ascend for the remainder of the day. None of the other dogs would make friends with so sour a fellow. Perhaps he was only oversensitive and introspective, and I do him wrong. I fear, however, that he will be sent to the penitentiary at Forty Mile for a long term one of these days.

Shorty, the end dog (wheel horse) of the husky team, was born in Spitzbergen, where dogs are so white that when they are on a background of snow you know of their presence only by the black spots for their eyes and a bigger black spot for their noses. An equality in breadth and length gave Shorty his name. Like some fat old gentlemen whom we meet at the club, he was the more comical because he was unconsciously so. He didn't believe in being a martyr, and he always carried his head so that one of his eyes was on Jack. When the master was about to touch up Jack and Tommy, Shorty would begin suddenly to pull very hard. His legs were so short and his body was so chunky that if the team turned a sharp corner around a cake of ice he would often roll over like a ball of fur; or, in trying to keep up he would slip and fall down a fissure, hanging suspended by his collar while he looked around at Jack, saying:

"Oh, I know I'm the snapper of the whip! What next?"

He blinked so oddly, there was such an expression of disgust in the very way in which he lolled his tongue out, that you laughed at him as you would at the old gentleman who finds another club member in his favorite chair and reading his favorite paper.

ON THE TRAIL

Tim, the larger of the two St. Bernards, was a sober, phlegmatic dog of noble mien, who was funny only when he ate so much porridge after a hard day's work that he groaned with pain.

"You needn't look at me so reproachfully, Tim," Jack would say, "I know I'm to blame. But I'd feel just as mean if I didn't feed you all you wanted."

The St. Bernard is too high-spirited for the work of a draught animal. At first Patsy seemed the better dog of the two. But Patsy wore himself out by fidgeting, and then it was his turn to soldier while Tim did his work. Toward the last they were in such bad shape that we dared to put only fifty pounds on their sled.

In the neighborhood of Five Fingers we met a dozen stranded pilgrims whose desperate efforts to reach Dawson in the previous autumn had been put to naught by the summary approach of the arctic winter when they were within a few days of their destination. They had built cabins on the banks of the river, wherever their boats had been inextricably caught in a jam of ice, and settled down to the prospect of playing checkers and fighting off scurvy for eight months, until summer came. Of those who were unsuccessful in the battle, the most afflicted was an old forty-niner who accepted with better grace than any of the others a diet of spruce tea and rice, which he hoped would undo the work of too much bacon. A few prospect holes had been sunk without any reward except " colors," because, as they explained, they were, in keeping with their general ill luck, just outside of the gold belt. For selfish as well as sentimental reasons we were glad that these unfortunate fellows were not more numerous. We had always to tell them some of the news, and then to leave their hospitality rather offended despite our explanations that we could not afford to tarry with them for a day's rest when the trail was good.

At one of the cabins a boy of seventeen years hobbled out to the bank to greet us. He and his uncle had left Dawson for the coast in December, drawing their own sleds. Hardship had so affected his uncle's mind, as the story was told to me, that to escape from the country had become a brutal and selfish mania with him. He forced his nephew, even at the point of the revolver, it was said, to do all the work of making and breaking camp. The boy was so tired one night that he crawled under his blankets without changing his moccasins, which had become wet by the slush snow about the fire. He awoke in the morning with his feet frozen. When they were overtaken on the trail by a man with a dog team, the next afternoon, the boy, goaded on by his uncle, was plodding along on legs which were frozen stiff up to his knees, experiencing, he said, much inconvenience but no pain. The fellow-traveller gave him a ride behind the dogs to the nearest cabin, where, later, a doctor on his way to the coast found amputation necessary to save the boy's life. As for the uncle, he delayed only a few hours, and hastened on his journey more energetically than ever.

A little hunting had been done by the stranded pilgrims, but with no success. We had hoped to obtain some venison from the Indians, but though we passed many of their deserted camps between the Hootalinqua and the Pelly, we came to only one that was occupied. Here two families were sitting around a small fire with their backs protected on all sides from the wind by a wall of brush about waist high. We secured a few pounds of extremely tough steak in exchange for some cornmeal. A small boy who looked quite like a young Jap knew a few English words and had the gift of making comprehensible gestures. He explained that he had heard his father's gun go "boom!" far off on the mountain-side, a few hours before. No chaffing could shake his confidence in his father, whose name was Chook, as a great hunter. One boom, he told us by signs, and the moose or caribou always tumbled over into the snow. The temptation to wait and see if Chook would return with fresh moose or caribou meat was great, but we resisted it. When, however, we were at the other end of the semicircle formed by the curve of the river beyond the camp, a cry from the bank showed us Chook, who had hastened through the woods by a trail known to himself, bearing a fine caribou steak and a piece of liver. With him, besides the little boy we had seen, was an elder brother who had been out to learn the way in which Daddy crept up quietly until he was within a few steps of his prey. Chook wanted sugar in exchange, but we had none to spare. Finally his obduracy was overcome and he accepted corn-meal. Long after we had passed on, he stood watching us, and presumably he was grinning over his bargain. We enjoyed part of the steak; Jack, the pup, stole the rest with such finesse that we forgave him.

When we had passed one point which we recognized as a name on the map, we looked forward from day to day, as we lessened the distance, until we should arrive at another. In camp we compared our opinions of how many miles we had made that day, and soon our estimates became surprisingly accurate. After leaving Five Fingers, all our thoughts were bent on reaching Fort Selkirk, where the Pelly, a great river of itself, joins the Yukon. The trail for this distance was better than for the fifty miles that had preceded it and the colder weather made sledging better. Moreover, our new plan of shorter hours and harder work was succeeding admirably.

Long before placer mining was thought of in Alaska or in the British Northwest Territory, representatives of the fur companies were stationed at Fort Selkirk. The present post is across the river from the upper ramparts of the Yukon's bank, whose towering walls of rock resemble the walls of old-time forts, even to the embrasures. In a break in the ramparts is the mouth of the Pelly, which is to the Yukon what the Missouri is to the Mississippi.

Mr. Pettit, the trader at Selkirk, had only Indians for companions. The aspect of this little man's loneliness was heightened by his slight form and his pallor, so out of place in a country where bare existence is supposed to demand so much vigor. In summer he busied himself with a little garden, which was an absorbing occupation because upon its success there possibly depended immunity from the dreaded scurvy. In winter he sat by his stove smoking when he was not sleeping. Watching the Indians go through the ritual of the Russian Church in their original manner, or dance around a dying fellow to keep off the evil spirit of death, were diversions which must by this time have lost their novelty for him. He had had nothing to sell for more than a year. This was a great disappointment to his customers who were short of those great requirements of aboriginal happiness, tobacco, sugar, and gay-colored clothes.

While we were at Pelly, the Indians became excited over the arrival of news that one of the tribe, Ulick, had shot ten caribou and two moose, "one sleep"—or more than a day's travel—down the river. We made careful calculations as to how much tobacco we could spare, and kept a sharp lookout for Ulick, whom we met with his family dragging some of the moose back to camp. For forty-five cents' worth of tobacco we secured thirty pounds of steak for ourselves and the dogs. To offers of as high as a dollar a pound for more, he merely made the reply :

"Got heap money! Want 'baccy!'"

Your husky dog is no vegetarian. Once we realized how much additional pulling-power our team could get out of a little fresh meat we denied ourselves for them.

The height and the character of the mountains towering over our heads told us that we were coming into the region of the Rockies. Every turn of the river brought into view a panorama of low wooded islands made in later times by a change of current; of islands that were Cyclopean masses thrown up by chaos, and the nesting-places of eagles; of mountains on either shore, whose strata seemed to have been kneaded and stirred when soft as dough, and afterward, upon solidifying, to have been rent by convulsions of the earth's crust.

But one was too busy with the handles of

the sled fully to enjoy scenery. You only knew that the vista seemed to be frowning upon the impudence of you and your sled and dogs breaking in upon great solitudes. Thankfully, the weather was more in our favor and the trail was harder, as it had been between the Big Salmon and Pelly, and not so sliding. At times it was as smooth as a skating-rink for a few hundred yards where it was protected from the sun by the shadow of the mountains and the forests; again, there was glare ice, where we might ride for a little distance, jesting merrily about private equipages and driving-parks; and, again, we drove flocks of wild ducks away from open places, making us regret that we had only revolvers with us. Far over our heads against the background of the blue sky we saw great flocks of wild swans and wild geese moving northward in stately procession, reminding us that summer was near at hand. At 2 A.M. the thermometer was at from 10 to 20 degrees below zero; at noon, 80 degrees above, and the crust of dawn had become like porridge. I had one ear blistered by the frost and the other by the sun in the same day.

But we little minded these extremes; for the trail continued to be good, until one morning we arrived at the cluster of cabins called Stewart City, at the mouth of the Stewart River, where we rested for a day. Of the inmates of the cabins we bought enough rice to piece out the rations of our dogs.

A mile out of Stewart we met Anders, of Bay City, Michigan, who was drawing his own sled as he swung along in great strides in the company of an elderly man who had one dog. An idea for making a fortune had occurred to him and to carry it out he had started for Dyea at once, regardless of the season of the year. He was "going outside" to bring in the stock for a poultry farm which he proposed to establish on an island near Dawson.

"Fresh eggs will bring ten dollars a dozen any time," he said, "and a spring chicken as much. I ain't going to let anybody get ahead of me, you bet. I've got a side of bacon and a sack of flour. I'll sleep by day and go without a blanket. I'll make it to Five Fingers with my sled and then I'll take what's left of my grub on my back and skin along the shore till I get to the lakes, where I can get some more grub off the boats that are coming in, snake a canoe somewhere, and paddle up to Linderman."

I saw him in Dawson two weeks after the pilgrims' flotilla began to arrive. The ice in the river had broken before he reached Five Fingers. He had climbed over mountains and beaten his way through underbrush until he sprained his ankle. Then he crawled to a ledge of rock overlooking the stream and waited until a pilgrim in a passing boat saw the red bandanna which he waved as a signal of distress.

"And I guess Dawson won't have turkey for Thanksgiving this year," he added. "You remember the old feller that was with me? We got separated. He couldn't keep up with my gait. Well, our boat passed his dog running up and down the shore howling, but we couldn't find a sign of him. I guess he was drowned."

It took us six days to make the remaining seventy-five miles to Dawson, though now our outfit, including bedding and kit-bags, did not weigh more than two hundred pounds. The weather at night had suddenly moderated, as if the arctic winter, after a spasmodic resistance, had given way entirely to the tropical summer. Henceforth, it was needless to put up our tent, and we slept and cooked entirely

The First Boats.

in the open, drying our wet footwear by the heat of the sun in the late afternoon.

Starting at 2 A.M. with the first light, we plodded straight ahead through the snow up to our knees, until the dogs gave out. We followed the trail where we could; followed it until it led us to the flowing river, and then we made a detour around the open place. The snow-shoes which we had brought thus far without having once put them on, now became invaluable in making a path by slow and arduous tramping, as monotonous as the beating of time, but a little more tiring, I assure you. Without the relief of the color of the dogs or of the man in front of you upon which to rest your eyes, little red spots would dance in the glare on the snow even through heavy green glasses. Often the rest of the party had to wait while Jack, who never tired, went on ahead to see if, in case we should go around this or that island, we should be obliged to retrace our steps. Again, in little side channels where the water was deep only in a freshet, we hitched all the dogs to one sled at a time and they dragged it over the sandy bottom and up on the other side, where we were likely to strike out on an old Indian trail bare of snow, and to have to lift the sleds from side to side to avoid saplings.

It was our boast that only once had we unpacked the sleds except to make camp. This was at Five Fingers, where we had to carry our baggage piece by piece up an ascent of forty feet. Even there we had sent the dogs up with the small sled on bare ground. But now we could lift the sleds and contents; or if the bank or ledge of rocks which we wished to gain was very precipitate, we could slide them up on skids. Dude, the old leader, would crawl up by himself without a whine, like a true soldier. Jack threw the other huskies up bodily, and the clumsy St. Bernards were pushed and pulled and coaxed up.

Just when we had to undergo the greatest physical labor, and the greatest strain from climate, our food-supply, so astonishing had been our appetites, had dwindled to flour and bad bacon, and we had remaining only a pipe of tobacco apiece, which was religiously saved for our last camp. We missed most keenly our chocolate, of which we had eaten half a pound apiece a day. With a slab of it for luncheon, and only two flapjacks and a slice of bacon, we were not hungry again for five or six hours. Consume all the flapjacks and bacon that we could without suffering from that excess of quantity which is the foe of exercise, in three or four hours our stomachs would be calling for more.

On the afternoon of the fourth day out from Stewart, when the dogs pulled up after one of the rushes they were never too tired to make on scenting a camp, we looked up to see some figures standing on a pile of logs which they were cutting for a raft of timber for a Dawson saw-mill.

"How are ye?" they called. "Goin' to town?"

We had reached the suburbs!

"Well," replied Jack, "we've been thinkin' some of it. How far is it?"

"'Bout twenty miles. But you won't make it. The ice is likely to go out any minute."

On the day following we passed still another camp of rafters, who said that the river was open in front of Dawson. They advised us to make camp and accompany them when navition opened.

"We'll be old inhabitants by that time," said Jack.

Every creek flowing into the river was a

torrent, eating up the ice and flooding its surface. We could see that the river was rising, which was a sure sign that its days were few. However, we were confident of reaching our destination on the morrow, though we had to desert our sleds, put some flapjacks and slices of bacon in our pockets, and climb over the mountain which hid "town" from view.

Our last camp was on a wooded island where some prospector had built a brush-house. Jack's bonfire, especially large in honor of the occasion, extended to this house, and we thought it rather good fun that we had to save our bedding from the flames. But our jubilation was not unmixed with sadness. We should not make another journey together, and we had been good comrades, always venting our anger, when it insisted upon expression, upon our sleds, and never blaming one another.

Our hair and beards were long and unkempt; our trousers were the color of mahogany; but we felt strong enough to go up the side of a mountain on the run, and we had been so near to nature that we could truly claim her for next-door neighbor.

In the future, the numerous police stations built in the summer (1898) will furnish food for travellers and their dogs. Already, therefore, our journey in the manner that we made it is a thing of the past, and, accordingly, one feels as he looks back on it a little of the pride of the pioneer.

"We can sleep as long as we want, to-morrow," said Fritz, pulling his robe over him, "and we won't care whether it is going to freeze at night or not."

"And we won't have wet feet," Jack added. "I guess it's been twenty days since they wasn't sopping 'fore we'd been out two hours, and that slush does feel rather clammy when the sun's blisterin' overhead."

Ten miles in ten hours was the record of our last day's travel, over the worst trail we had encountered. At dusk we rounded an island, and to our right, on a small flat across the river (which here had been opened by the current of the Klondyke), we saw the cluster of cabins which was the pilgrim's Mecca. There was glare ice, however, above the Klondyke across to the little suburb of Dawson, Klondyke City. For the first time in many days we rode on our sleds, finishing our journey in triumph.

"Don't you know that it's too late to travel

on the river?" asked the foremost man of the little crowd that came out to meet us.

"Yes," replied Jack, "and we've just made up our minds to quit."

Four days later, as if it had broken away all along the shores at the same moment, the ice moved on toward the sea like a great white procession, halted now and then by a jam, but not for long.

"It's a pleasure to see that trail go by," was Jack's comment, as he watched it from our cabin-door. "I only wish I might pay it back in its own kind by tripping it up a few times."

III

DAWSON

SOCIAL ASPECTS OF DAWSON — CORNERING THE TINNED FOOD MARKET — CHEECHAWKOS AND OLD-TIMERS IN THE EARLY DAYS.

AT this season of the year the inhabitants of Dawson were passing out of the chrysalis of fur caps into soiled, broad-brimmed hats resurrected from cabin-shelves; out of winter clothing generally into what remained of their last summer's clothing. Along the thawing bog called the main street, littered and odorous from sanitary neglect, were two rows of saloons and gambling-halls, with mining-brokers' offices and the stores of shrewd speculators in food-supplies, who always had one can of condensed milk for $2.50, one can of butter for $5, and one pound of sugar for $1.50, and assured you that they were the last in the country. To look out across the flat toward the mountains was to see scattered cabins and piles of tin cans, which at once let one into the culinary secrets of an isolated community composed largely of men. At the restaurants, bacon and beans and coffee cost $2.50.

For a time in the winter in fear of famine the well-to-do hoarded food as they hoard gold in a financial panic, and the restaurants were closed because supplies were not procurable at prices that made catering profitable. Then, a fifty-pound sack of flour sold for as high as $100; but at the approach of spring the little capitalists who had planned to sell their "corners" at great profit were glad enough to dispose of such surplus as they had beyond their own needs at a loss. To them the departure of hundreds of mouths which otherwise would have been fed out of Dawson's granary was as great a disappointment as a report that Hungary's wheat crop would greatly exceed expectations is to the bulls on the Chicago Exchange. All of the luxuries and many of the necessities of life were scarce; but, withal, there was quite enough of bacon, beans, and flour to have satisfied the appetites of the whole community for a month after supplies arrived. According to the philosophy of the old-timers, there is never any danger of a man's starving as long as he will look ahead a little.

So easy is it to sleep and so little does one eat when one is not working that he can live on a pound of food a day, if need be, and take the remainder of his nourishment in slumber. On the other hand, vigorous labor in winter demands at least three pounds a day, and it is upon this basis that estimates have always been made in the valley of the Yukon.

With a tiny can of cocoa, which I pounced upon in a store as if it were an Elzevir in a junk-heap, and a few staples bought at extravagant prices, we were able to prepare a superior meal in the cabin that I had leased. But this was not until we had slept gloriously for sixteen hours. There remained the problem of a bath, which was serious, as the one bath-house in Dawson was closed for repairs. I solved it legitimately, if uncomfortably, in the wooden tub which was lent to me by a neighbor.

The saloons had only a substitute for whiskey, of home manufacture. The dance-halls were not open. All the men whose dust and presence would make the camp lively were at the mines—or "up the creeks," as the saying goes in Dawson—preparing for the "clean-up."

In winter and in summer the trail leads up the Klondyke to the mouth of Bonanza, three miles from Dawson, and thence up Bonanza to the working-claims, about three miles farther on. In the spring, when the currents are swollen, you must go over a high mountain by a path in the soft snow. If you have a pack, this is hard work. On the way I met a blue-faced old fellow—by his look if not by his limp he had the scurvy—who promptly put me in my proper social status.

"Are ye a Cheechawko?" he asked.

"I don't know, I'm sure."

"Well, then, ye are, and the river must 'a' broke. Any man's a Cheechawko until he's been in the country when the ice goes out. In the old days we could lick the Cheechawkos into shape; larn 'em to leave their latch-strings out fur a passin' stranger when they was away from hum, and larn 'em to eat what they wanted and to use the best blanket in a cabin, but to lug nothin' away. Fifty thousand of 'em, they say—clerks and farmers and dudes. They're too many fur us. Civilization's here, and it's a case of locking up yer dust after this. But, young man, ye can't be an old-timer, never! Ye can't be an old-timer, 'less ye've lived in the camps in the old days when a man was a man and his neighbor's brother."

And without giving me time to reply to his little lecture, he hobbled on toward the hospital.

Cheechawko is the Indian word for stranger, or, more literally, tenderfoot, which has come into general use in the Klondyke; and toward the Cheechawko, bringing in the more penurious ways of the outside world, along with ignorance of mining, the old-timer feels a genuine resentment. I was glad of the opportunity to see the veterans ere the recruits had arrived.

IV

THE FIRST DISCOVERIES

The Beginning of Mining in Alaska—Forty Mile Creek—Canadian and American Deposits—The Largest Log-Cabin Town in the World—Life of the First Adventurers — The Superfluity of Six-Shooters — Leaving the Latch-Strings Out — The Way of the Transgressors—Indian Charley and his Nugget.

A LITTLE history of placer mining in the Yukon valley, at this turn of my narrative, will be of importance, I think, in making what follows more comprehensible. It was early in the eighties, if not before, that the first prospectors, armed with Indian tales, faith, and a "gold pan," packed their supplies to the shores of the Lewes lakes over the passes which were the means of communication between the Indians of the coast and those of the interior. They followed the ice out of the lakes and down the river into a practically unexplored country, panning out of the gravel at the mouth of each tributary.

At first, these and the other brave spirits who

A Typical Pilgrims' Boat.

THE FIRST DISCOVERIES

were encouraged to follow their example arduously poled their boats back up-stream in September, with the result of their summer's labor, to spend the winter in one of the towns of the quartz-mining region in southeastern Alaska or in the Pacific Coast States. Some had three or four hundred dollars; others, who had impatiently disregarded certain "pay" on the bars of the tributaries and had prospected in the hope of making a great "strike," returned with little or nothing.

Soon they began to take in enough supplies to last them through the winter, and to build cabins for their protection. A little settlement sprang up on the site of the "diggings" of Forty Mile Creek. All of the rich deposits thus far have been found not on the tributaries of the Yukon but on the tributaries of the tributaries. (The wealth of the far-famed Klondyke is not on the Klondyke River but on Eldorado and Bonanza, which flow into it.) So the next progressive step was a discovery which led to the working of the frozen ground in the valleys of the numerous little streams tributary to Forty Mile, by stripping off the dirt as fast as the very hot sun of the long days of the arctic summer thawed it. This process, however, was feasible only when the "pay-dirt" was near to the surface, and the season of activity was still restricted to four or five months of the year.

As the prospectors moved on down the river, gradually widening the circle of their labors and their experience, deposits considerably richer than those of the tributaries of Forty Mile were found on the tributaries of Birch Creek in American territory. Here, for the first time, an innovation, which did not appeal to everybody, made it feasible to work twelve months in the year. An energetic man sank a shaft to bedrock with fires. Then he drifted out his "pay-dirt" in the same manner and piled it in dumps on the surface to be sluiced out in summer. By the autumn of 1896, when the great discovery of Bonanza Creek was made, Circle City was said to be the largest log-cabin town in the world, and from twenty-five hundred to three thousand white men dwelt in the Yukon valley.

Experience in placer mining counted for little in a region where conditions were so different from those of the Pacific Coast States. There was no sprinkling of capitalists or mining engineers among those robust pilgrims of the early days. Many of the hardships which they endured are already a memory. They were cheered in their combat with nature by no such tales as lured on the Cheechawkos of 1897-98. The majority of them came from the frontiers of the United States; a smaller part, generally of French descent, from the frontiers of Canada. All were peculiarly the product of the Anglo-Saxon bent for overcoming obstacles. Not infrequently there were fugitives from justice, who, having the inclination and the energy to undergo great physical trials rather than serve a term in prison, and learning a lesson in manhood by bitter retrospection, have often become heroic pioneers. More numerous than the inhabitants of the old centres of civilization would suppose were those recluses who are ever seeking lonely refuges out of touch with the advance posts of organized society.

There was no prospect, especially when no "big strikes" had been reported, to attract the idle and the dissolute who infest similar settlements in more hospitable countries. Relieved of the parasitic class and being interdependent in isolation from the outside world under the most rigorous conditions for eight months in the year, their inhabitants, despite the " pasts " of some of them, made Circle City and Forty Mile the most peaceable of mining camps. Captain Constantine, of the British Northwest Mounted Police, with a few men, had plenary powers at Forty Mile, while Circle City was nominally governed by a United States Commissioner and a United States Marshal.

All the white women in both communities could be counted on the fingers of two hands. Mrs. Constantine, the wives of a few missionaries and of a few leading men, had come in on steamers up the river in summer to join their husbands. Half a dozen half-breed women, with more or less of the blood of Russian fur traders in their veins, composed the demi-monde of either camp. Full-blooded squaws performed the household duties in some cabins for a civilized lord and master. But the " squaw man " was the exception. In no part of the world where isolated white men live among aborigines was the man who had a native mistress held in greater disrespect than here.

As a rule, the miners did their own washing and mending. Their amusements were card-playing and checker-playing. The climate seemed to exercise a softening effect upon bellicose natures, and even intoxication seldom carried quarrels beyond a dispute of words. Whoever struck the first blow had the consensus of opinion of the camp against him.

"We've got enough to do fighting Alaska," was a saying which sententiously expressed the general feeling, "without fighting one another."

To the new-comer it was hinted that a six-shooter, which fiction makes the inseparable companion of all men in a new placer mining camp, was a superfluity that would keep him out of trouble only when he kept it at all times hanging on a peg in his cabin. Its weight alone was equal to two days' rations in a country where the prospector had to dispense with his helpmeet, the mule or the burro, and carry his grub for a tour on his back. Therefore, arms were never carried unless there was a chance of meeting with game.

The essence of the "free miners' law" was being on the "squar'," which, after all, is a rough equivalent of the brotherhood of man. Between the disputants as to the ownership of a claim the "miners' meeting" decided which one was in the right. All offenders were brought before the bar of their fellows. A man accused of theft, after an examination of witnesses, was acquitted or convicted by the holding up of hands. If guilty, he was, according to the circumstances, either warned to leave the country for good—no slight penalty in midwinter with only the hospitality of Indians to depend upon—or else ostracism was postponed pending good behavior. "Miners' meeting law" is unscientific and rarely commendable, but here it served its purpose well because its methods made it so seldom required.

Under the force of self-interest a universal good-will prevailed. Whatever a miner had —perhaps the increment of a summer's earnings which was to pay for another year's supplies—he kept in tomato cans on the table of his cabin with impunity. When he went away from home on a journey to some other creek he left his latch-string out. On the very evening of his absence, while his cabin was occupied by another, he was, perhaps, sleeping in someone else's without an invitation. By the unwritten law of the land he enjoyed whatever luxuries of food and rest the cabin

THE FIRST DISCOVERIES

afforded; but, likewise by the unwritten law of the land, he washed any dishes that he had used and put them and all other things that he had disturbed back where they belonged, folded the blankets on the bunk, cut firewood in place of that which he had burned, and laid kindlings by the stove ready to make warmth and cheer for the owner when he should return, cold and weary.

Cheechawkos who came down the river in the spring in their rough boats at first, through ignorance, were often transgressors of the unwritten laws. But so few arrived at a time that the majority were soon able to convince them of the folly of courting trouble for themselves. Anyone with a bad record could not obtain favors or a loan when he needed it. After he had consumed the supplies which he had brought into the country with him, he must rely upon the transportation companies, established to meet the demand of the new settlements, whose river steamers connected with ocean-going vessels at the island of St. Michael in Norton Sound. When a man had been unfortunate in his summer's work, a reputation for probity would secure from the companies a year's outfit on a simple promise to pay. In treating generously the real prospector who sought new fields, they only had an eye to their own interests in the development of the country. Every canned and preserved delicacy was included in a year's supplies, costing from $500 to $600. Canned plum pudding was a treat for the holidays; and more than one miner ate *pâté de foie gras* for the first time in Circle City or Forty Mile. These luxuries, however, were no substitutes for fresh fruits and fresh vegetables.

The flat-bottomed river steamers continued on their course until the ice in the river led them to seek a slough or side channel for safety, all hands preparing to spend the winter housed up on board. Then no more Cheechawkos' boats could arrive, and the camps were as completely separated from the outside world as a whaler caught in the ice of Bering Sea. To all men, including the recluses, a "pardner" was essential. For the recluses were recluses from civilization and not from fellow-men of their own tastes; and no one, except a few of the most perverse, undertook single-handed to put up a cabin or to live in it alone.

The "town" was on the river bank at the

most accessible point to the creeks whose wealth was responsible for its existence. Its cabins clustered around the commercial companies' stores and the saloons. To one side was a camp of Indians and the mission station which ministered to their spiritual wants and, following the paths of diplomacy, to the spiritual wants of the miners—upon request. Fuel was brought from the hill-sides and food was taken to the cabins on the creeks by teams of husky dogs.

When the winter settled down in serene triumph in December there was not even the falling of snow to disturb the calm atmosphere. The fine white particles under foot, which seemed as sharp as powdered glass to the touch, were precipitated invisibly, like frost. They glistened on the mountain-sides without a breath of air to stir them. In the few hours of gray light out of the twenty-four, men welcomed the sound of their own voices, or even the howl of their dogs, to break the silence which was the fit companion of the dry, biting cold. At night they forgave the still and merciless panorama of the day as they watched out of their cabin-windows the play of the Northern Lights, in which nature has furnished for the eyes a greater treat than is the breaking of surf for the ears.

With the coming of spring, when the sun mounted so rapidly in the heavens, every man had his opinion and his reasons for it as to the exact date when the ice should go out of the Yukon. After this—the greatest event of the year—had taken place, all eyes kept a lookout up-stream for the first pine-colored boat that should dart around the bend with the rapidity of the current. The Cheechawko was surrounded by a little crowd which asked him about the result of the previous November's elections, or if France and Germany had gone to war as indicated by an August paper which the community had been reading for eight months.

As a rule, the early arrivals had been in the country before. They knew the channels and the currents of the river, and could resist the temptation of stopping to pan the gravel of the bars in search of colors, for the old-timers had long since concluded that the travel-worn particles of dust to be found at the mouths of all of the tributaries of the Yukon which are in the so-called gold belt, were vagrants and not the advance guard of a floating pilgrim-

THE FIRST DISCOVERIES

age. They had poled weary miles in their long boats and carried packs for wearier ones without finding at the head-waters of the tributaries, which were named by them and still await accurate mapping by geographers, any original deposits. The shallow bedrock in the neighborhood of Forty Mile put the original deposits there within reach of the summer's sun and the superficial investigation of the hurrying prospector, and opened the way to the discovery of richer original deposits at Circle City at a slightly greater depth of bedrock.

So the miners had concluded that the next great strike, following the progress of development down the river, would be made below Circle City. On account of an Indian's keen glance the contrary happened, and they retraced their footsteps to find fortunes at a depth of thirty feet under soil whose surface they had trod before. The sharp-eyed Indian was a brother-in-law of "Siawash George," and "Siawash George" was an outcast, whose nickname was given to him by his fellow white men. The Siawashes are one of the lowest orders of the American Indians, and the old-timers, so largely men from the Pacific Coast, use Siawash both as a noun and as an adjective to signify contempt. One of the first white pilgrims to cross the passes, Cormac, was now the father of three or four half-breed children. He had planned that his marriage to a princess of the tribe would be the stepping-stone of his ambition to become chief of the Sticks. In the autumn of 1896 he and his family and retainers were encamped at the mouth of the Klondyke, gathering from the land and the water, according to aboriginal custom but with modern riffles and hooks, their winter supply of provender.

The Klondyke is one of the best rivers in the neighborhood for fish, much better than the Indian River, which flows into the Yukon between thirty and forty miles above it. At the summit of the water-shed between the Indian and the Klondyke is a great mountain, which, from its shape, the miners have named The Dome. In the snows of its sides six creeks have their origin, three flowing into either stream. The longest of these is sixteen miles. They wind through beds of black muck, ranging from fifty to two hundred and fifty yards in breadth, which lie between steep embankments. It is presumed that the em-

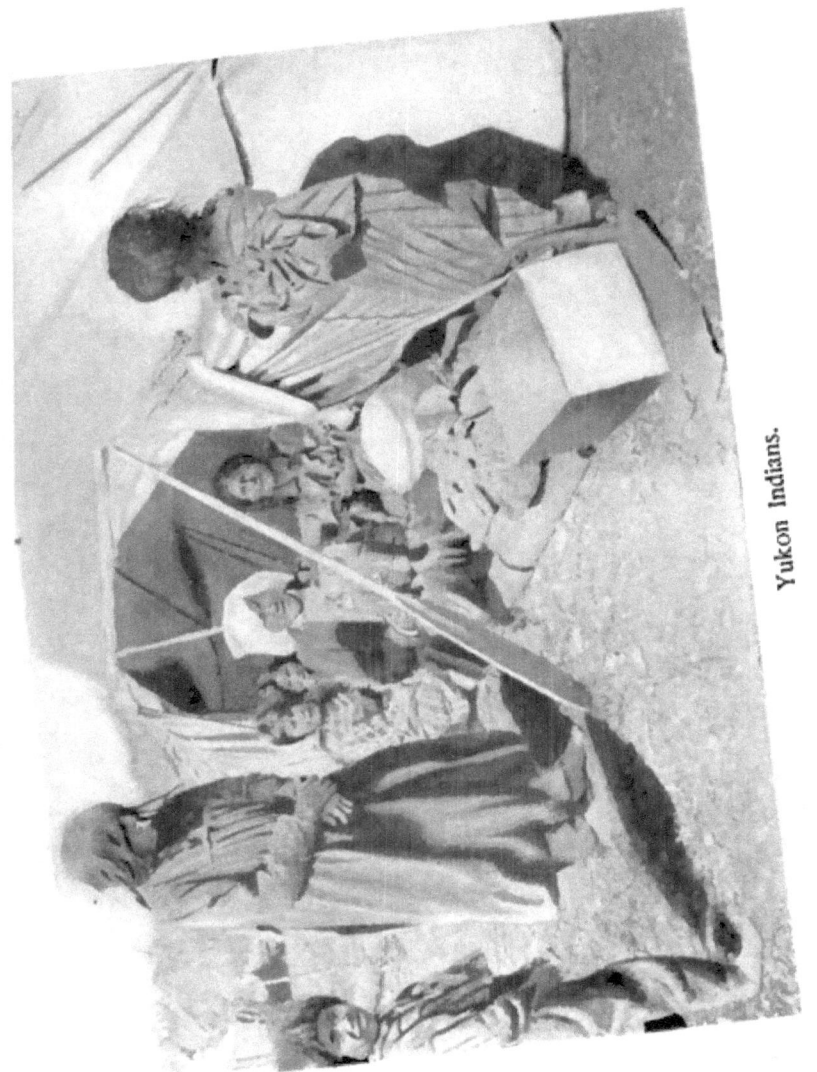

Yukon Indians.

THE FIRST DISCOVERIES

bankments are the walls of an ancient river channel. They are indented only by the gulches cut by tributaries which once were mighty but now have dwindled to little torrents which flourish only with the first warmth of spring or after a heavy rain in summer. The great heat of June, July, and August drew out of the muck with a growth of tropical rapidity a rank grass upon which the moose fed in peace, fattening his sides, made lean by winter's privations.

Here "Injun Sharley," as he called himself, came to look for moose, and here he found instead, as he was crossing the first tributary of the Klondyke at a point where its bending course had dug a niche out of the side-hill, a glistening nugget of gold. According to all of the preconceived ideas of the placer mining prospectors, no creeks in the region were so unpromising as these. Those few prospectors who had tramped up this valley, finding a few colors in the shoals made by washing the earth of the embankment, had passed them by with the ever-ready expression of the country:

"Oh, well, you can find colors anywhere."

If the turn of the creek had not washed one stray nugget as well as stray colors out of a bench which no one found worth working two years after discovery, the moose might still be feeding undisturbed in the valleys of Eldorado and Bonanza creeks, which are now as expressive of man's handiwork as the rear of a row of tenement houses, and certain unhappy newspaper correspondents would not have missed the Spanish-American War.

There is no reason to believe that "Siawash George," personally, had any great confidence in the "strike." Rather—after having staked creek claims for himself and "Injun Sharley"—he thought it worth advertising, when advertising was so cheap because of the expert canoists and good pedestrians in his family. He was further assisted in spreading the news by Joe La Due, another "squaw man," who has been erroneously called Father of the Klondyke, just as "Siawash George," and not "Injun Sharley," has been called its discoverer. La Due staked out a town-site on the flat which had been formed in the course of time by the alluvial deposits of the Klondyke at its mouth. He was fond of "booms," and as a part of his plan of promoting his latest boom he offered lots for five dollars apiece to all who would stake claims on the new creeks. Neither

THE FIRST DISCOVERIES

he nor "Siawash George" had much to lose and they might gain a great deal if shafts were sunk to bedrock with fires after the plan that had lately come into vogue at Circle City.

When an Indian arrived at Forty Mile and then at Circle City with a tale out of all proportion to the actual size of the nugget that "Injun Sharley" had found, the miners received it with that garlic cynicism which has its natural abiding-place in the unkempt beards of hardened frontiersmen. They had become so used to strikes with no foundation except an irresponsible imagination, as nominally to believe in nothing that a man said about any find he had made. So they told the Indian that he was a liar pure and simple, who had been primed by an ambitious brother-in-law. The Indian had been told to expect this reply and was not the least disturbed in mind by it. But no miner acts upon his convictions in such a matter. He usually hurries off to the reported scene of the find because, after all, "mebbe there might be somethin' in it." But such were the reputations of Joe La Due and Cormac that many of the earlier pioneers refused to budge. Their superior wisdom was as unfortunate for them as absence from the settlements was for those at work on the creeks. The two or three hundred, lounging in the saloons and the stores or resting in their cabins, who made for the mouth of the Klondyke in the mood of men who are playing a joke on themselves, became rich.

There were not enough claims on the discovery creek, Bonanza, for all of them, so the later arrivals, just for the sake of staking something, contemptuously staked a tributary of Bonanza, which they called in their phrase a "pup." Then there was naught to do but to wait until a few of the more energetic fellows sunk holes on Bonanza. No one was more surprised at the result than "Siawash George." Bedrock on Bonanza showed the richest placer dirt yet found in Alaska or the British Northwest Territory. Those who had been in time to stake claims on Bonanza settled down to work at once, incidentally extending their pity to the fellows on the "pup." The claim-owners on Eldorado, where no shaft had been sunk, accepted the pity in good part and offered their claims at various prices, ranging from one hundred to five hundred dollars. Most of them were so lucky as to be unable to make a sale, and are now worth from five hundred thousand

THE FIRST DISCOVERIES

to a million dollars apiece. The "pup" is the richest placer mining creek in the world.

Nine months after "Injun Sharley" had brought home a nugget instead of a moose, the outside world heard of the great discovery. Such pilgrims, attracted by the news, as succeeded in reaching Dawson in the autumn of 1897 found that all creeks rising on the slopes of The Dome and all other creeks at that time proven to be worth the working, had already been staked by the old-timers who had followed the advance guard from Circle City and Forty Mile. Feverish stampede followed on feverish stampede to new ground. That putting down four stakes in a creek-bed anywhere in the region was equal to drawing a fortune from a bank became the gospel of the hour, which received its authority from the original attitude toward the "pup" of the men who had staked Eldorado. A man needed only to come into a saloon with a pack on his back, and, being tired, appear silent and mysterious, to excite the suspicion that he had made a "strike." "Only an affidavit" of having found "color" was necessary to have a discovery claim recorded, and a discovery always meant a stampede. Having received a hint from a friend, or overheard a whispered conversation in the street, a pilgrim would rush off for a distance of more than a day's travel, without food or blankets, trusting to luck to feed him and keep him warm. Death was often the result.

Having staked the remaining creeks in a radius of from thirty to sixty miles of Dawson, some of the new-comers rested in their cabins, eating their winter's supply of food. Others found employment on the work-claims; and still others departed over the ice to escape starvation and to thrill their neighbors at home with the information that they owned claims. As the humor of the saloons went, there remained for the oncoming host of May and June an expanse of unexplored territory sufficient to keep a hundred times their number busy prospecting for a century, but no gold at all, unless they could find it for themselves.

V

MINERS AND MINING

Reaping the Gold Harvest—Thawing and Sluicing—Miners and their Theories—The Dome—Expensive Timber—Empty Pockets but Dollars in the Dumps—The First Millionnaires—Color in the Pan—Once a Prospector Always a Prospector—Figuring Fortunes—Capitalists in Demand—The Forty Happy Kings on Eldorado.

IT was just on the eve of harvest-time when I first visited the creeks. In a day or two the flow of water from the gulches where the snow lay thickest would make a head sufficient to wash the yellow grain out of the dumps. Along the four miles of Eldorado, or its full length, and the ten miles of working claims on Bonanza, lines of flumes and their dependent sluice-boxes—the lumber for which had been drawn on sleds from Dawson by husky dogs, or cut with whipsaws—formed a network around the string of cabins occupied by claim-owners and their workmen and around the piles of clayish-colored dirt, thawed out inch by inch during the short winter days, which contained virgin wealth amounting to ten million dollars. The hill-sides, once covered with timber, were bare of all except stumps and scarred by broad streaks from top to bottom, showing where logs for building the cabins and for feeding the fires in the drifts had been slid down.

If you descended by the shafts beside the dumps to the drifts, you soon comprehended that reaping the harvest, once you have a claim, is not so easy as picking wild cranberries. It is dogged work to build fires day after day, running the risk of suffocation and permanent injury to the eyes by the smoke, and pulling up the dirt, bucketful after bucketful, by means of a windlass, with the thermometer forty below zero—and the prospect of cooking your own dinner. The rising steam from the thawing pay-dirt of the drifts, which fills the valley with mist, adds the discomfort of humidity to the biting cold. Though the man who turns the windlass may have to beat his hands and dance about to keep warm, he is never in positive danger as is his partner below, who, in returning to relight one of the series of nicely arranged piles of wood which have failed to ignite, is likely to be suffocated, or, barring such slips as this or any consequent accident, is sure to suffer continually from soreness and smarting of the eyes, if not to have them permanently injured by the smoke.

In one spot of three or four square feet on Eldorado, the nuggets are so thick that you can pick them out by hand as a farmer's boy picks potatoes out of a hill. In juxtaposition there may be as many more square feet which are not considered worth thawing and sluicing; and so the angles of the drifts seem like the path of a man of vacillating mind trying to make his way to the light in darkness. From two to three feet above the real bedrock is the false bedrock, a stratum of stone broken into angular fragments, apparently by some great force passing overhead. Between the two is the best paying-dirt, and occasionally here is found, perhaps with particles of gold sticking to it, the tusk of a mammoth who was the ruler in the valley before the days of the moose.

In the angular fragments of the false bedrock the miners who are fond of making out the reason of things over their cabin-fires, with diversified reading in newspapers or even a dip in a text-book of geology at school as basic knowledge, find support for their favorite theory as to how the yellow particles came to their resting-place. Gold had never been found before in such incongruous surroundings. Therefore, they contend, it must have been borne from its point of precipitation by some force worthy of the situation and of Alaska, where nature has a gift for seemingly paradoxical performances done on a Brobdingnagian scale. What else but a glacier was equal to the feat? It had scattered wealth in its progress like some good Lady Bountiful, crushing with its great weight the false bedrock between whose fragments the dust had fallen by force of gravity to the true bedrock.

Another, a smaller and perforce a more confident school of thought, holds that an ancient volcano "coughed" the dust out of the bowels of the earth.

For my part, inasmuch as the geologists themselves have come to no certain conclusion, I hold that all the gold which has been found in the Klondyke and Indian River districts was smelted in a great pot in The Dome and has leaked out of its cracks. Then, as a fitting corollary, I desire that one day an old forty-niner, as sturdy and as fine as an old weather-beaten oak, shall discover the pot and

On the Creeks.

find a leverage strong enough to lift the cover off it; whereupon, a good guardian, gently reserving enough of his millions to give him a certain annuity for life, he may spend the rest in 'Frisco after the manner of his own choosing as quickly as he can. But I am certain—such is the irony of fate—that, instead of him, the happy man will be an Oklahoma "boomer," the father of several strapping daughters, who never panned a handful of dirt before he mortgaged his all in order to buy a Klondyker's outfit. He will set his daughters up in the capitals of Europe, where they will marry continental noblemen, while the whole family will be miserable for life.

In candor, I must say that with mine as with most theories there are facts which go to contradict it. The claims on the upper reaches of the creeks, which have their origin on the slopes of The Dome, are much richer than those on the lower reaches, where the dust is finer and more travel-worn as well as more scattering. But in the head-waters nothing has yet been found which is worth the working. So either all the gold leaked out some time before this force that carried it ceased to operate, or the mythical person who has charge of the pot mended the cracks, or, possibly—and this is my hope—the fortunes which have already been brought to light were only an overflow, the palpable result of the chemist in charge of the vessel having misjudged its capacity.

By the fifteenth of May the drifts were filled or partly filled with seepage which had frozen below a depth of a few feet, where the temperature is never above freezing. Work in them was at an end by the first of May, when the surface earth had begun to thaw a little at midday. Then the plane, saw, and hammer took the place of the pick and shovel. If they had used rosewood at New York or London prices the miners could not have built their flumes and sluice-boxes out of more expensive material than that they had in the warping, knotty fir boards which were condescendingly sold at $250 a thousand by the three saw-mills in the country. Once the flumes were laid to the gulches and to the dams in the creek itself, the sluice-boxes were properly laid on the dumps which were to be washed first and the gates between the two were made tight, the community was ready to reap the reward of a winter's toil as soon as the sun should thaw the drifts of snow on the mountain-sides sufficiently to make a sluice-head of water.

There followed a brief period of inactivity like that between sowing and harvest for the farmer. Every man had his opinion of how much the output of all the creeks would be, and the estimates varied from six to fifteen millions. Within the big world of speculation there were the small worlds of the groups of cabins which clustered around that of the owner of each claim on Eldorado and Bonanza. For the laymen who had taken portions of claims to work on shares and for the claim-owners, especially those who had employed the workers on their claims at daily wages, it was an interval of some anxiety. They would soon know in what measure the estimates that they had made from specimens of pay-dirt panned out in buckets of water in their cabins during the winter would be verified. Men who had more than a hundred thousand dollars in their dumps possibly had not five dollars in cash in their possession.

The members of no community had ever been submitted to a greater burden of usury. They bore it with rare good-nature. What else were they to do? they asked. They needed money for wages, for food for their men, and for lumber, and those in town who had money knew the value of it. The regular rate in the winter was ten per cent. a month, and some of the so-called millionnaires who had owned nothing except an outfit two years before were owing as much as $25,000 on from three to six months' time.

A spirit of optimism and good cheer prevailed. A sun bath, lounging in a home-made chair on the stoop of a cabin (perhaps with a pair of moose horns forming an ornamental back), was a luxury better appreciated in the Klondyke than in a temperate clime. Sometimes a breeze, with a faint odor of fir-trees and of the many wild flowers which spring up in tropical luxuriance in the spring, came down the valley. Over the hills were young birches which yielded a delicious sap for the tapping. There was even gratitude to the tyrant windlass of the winter days in that it had supplied exercise, given an appetite, kept the blood circulating, and prevented the scurvy, which is to be dreaded only by the man who lounges in his cabin, does not wash himself, does not cook his food properly, and endeavors generally to imitate the bear. Nearly everyone could hope, if he did not expect, that his claim or his lay would turn out as well as he had estimated. At all events, he would have some spending money. He knew that the early boats from Lake Le Barge would bring in many luxuries just at the opportune moment when the "clean-up" was about finished and he might go to "town." He smacked his lips in anticipation of the day when he would have all the eggs that he could eat, regardless of their cost.

One day the sun suddenly beat down with great fierceness, which was unabated for several days. Then the water came gushing down the flumes in greater quantity than was needed, and the men picked up their picks and shovels again and began peeling off the dirt on the dumps and tossing it into the sluice-boxes. The warmth was prolonged through the night, so that the dirt continued to thaw as fast as they could strip it off, and on many claims—whose owners had foresight or were in luck, as one pleases to put it—there were two shifts working all the time except when, once or twice a day, the boxes were being "cleaned" of the accumulation of gold and the sand which sinks with it between the cleats. The snowdrifts were melting as if they were under a blowpipe. Even the tiny streams of the gulches become torrents, dams had to be opened, and some sluice-boxes floated away from their moorings. Only too soon was the loss of the wasted energy brought home. With the snow gone and rains and the seepage from the thawing surface the only source of water supply, the currents dwindled until many claims had not a single sluice-head. The claim-owners on the tributary Eldorado, with as much dirt to wash as the main stream Bonanza, particularly had cause to resent the prodigality of nature in expending all of its ammunition at once. Instead of having finished their washing in June as they had confidently expected, all through July they were measuring the head of water from hour to hour with the care of a physician feeling a patient's pulse.

When the "clean-up" of a day's shovelling was made, you might feast your eyes on the consummation of the harvest. The water was shut off and the cleats in the boxes were lifted and rinsed, leaving a residue which glistened with yellow particles. Just a small stream was turned on by the man at the water-gates, who was probably making the most of his rest from shovelling by smoking a pipe of cut plug, and then turned off again, or on a little more or off a little less, while the most expert miner on the claim pushed the speckled sand-pile back and forth with a common brush-broom until all the foreign particles had floated off, except a sprinkling of the heavy black sand which is invariably the companion of placer gold.

Three or four or five thousand dollars—perhaps ten or fifteen or twenty thousand if the "clean-up" be on Eldorado—which is three or four or five double handfuls, is put into a pan with an ordinary fire-shovel. The sight is bound to make your blood run faster and to color your reason with an epic enthusiasm. That little yellow pile, you know at a glance, will stand the test of chemicals. It must also accept the concrete responsibility for all the disappointments, sufferings, and deaths of the pilgrims on the trail and the worries of their friends and relatives at home. Once you have seen a "color" in the bottom of a pan with the black sand following it around like a faithful servant, you can never again be deceived by the glitter of any false gods. You would know it if you saw it between cobblestones on Broadway, or if it were no larger than a pin-head at the bottom of a trout-pool.

It is small wonder that once a man is a prospector, in good faith, not a child of a wild stampede, he is always a prospector. There is an heroic aspect, the more charming in contrast to the complexity of civilization, in going from creek to creek which have no place on the maps of geographical societies, taking a pan of dirt here and a pan of dirt there, breathing fresh air, a zest given to your exercise by the hope of success.

For the moment, the yellow pile makes you feel like seeking a claim of your own and harvesting its treasure for yourself. But when you look at the miry path along the base of the mountain by the creek-side, and think of following it with a pack on your back until it is no more, and a wilderness begins; of passing on over the mountains until you come to what you consider a likely place, and thawing through thirty feet of earth at a rate of a foot a day in the hap-hazard possibility of finding "pay-dirt," you conclude that the poetry of the thing can be better appreciated by sitting on someone else's dump.

Besides, as one who did a little prospecting

on his own account and is proud to say that he found a few "colors"—which is just what any-one else can do in the Klondyke region—I observed that the recent arrivals of Nestorian prospectors who took a delight in quoting to you from Emerson when their hands were reeking with clay and their gray locks were sticking through the crowns of old hats, do not like Alaska, though free to admit its material opportunities. They could not be weaned from the temperate climate and the skies of California, and were determined to return to their old stamping-grounds, where any honest prospector can get a grubstake from a speculative city man, and needs nothing more to make him happy and free.

After a few days' washing the hopes of most of the laymen were shattered; and so far as their peace of mind was concerned, the worst of it was that they had only their own lack of foresight to blame. They had learned that even in the Klondyke men do not make a practice of giving fortunes away to strangers—except to music-hall artistes—though, as in the centres of civilization, they often negotiated a bargain with an air of self-sacrifice which is an assumption of as much.

Such was the attitude of many of the claim-owners below the discovery claim on Bonanza and of a few above who had prospected their claims well enough to have some idea of what was in them. They concluded to let out their ground to be worked on shares, two men to each section, which is called a lay. Many, especially those who had come in with the little pilgrimage that reached Dawson in the autumn of '97, were enraptured over the chance of getting a portion of a claim on the original creek and not far from "discovery," at that.

The number of applications quite exceeded the number of lays to be let, and all through the winter the laymen on Bonanza were the envy of their fellows. The samples which they washed out in their cabins had the peculiarity of bringing promises up to original expectations, because the laymen had the weakness of selecting the samples from their best dirt. When the man who was in the drift came to one of those rare spots in the pay-streak of Lower Bonanza where he could see the tiny particles shining in the wall of earth like golden hoar-frost, he gleefully called out to his "pardner" at the windlass to take it into the cabin so they could see how much it ran to the bucket. In the evening the happy children, upon the result as a basis, quite overestimating the amount of dirt they had in their dumps, figured out small fortunes for themselves, spoke of the claim-owner as a good angel, hugged their knees fondly, as if they had materialized into dust, and saw brilliant pictures in their smoke rings.

In their letters, detailing their success to the folks at home, they promised their wives new gowns and their daughters pianos. They were doing so well that they felt that they could afford holidays. They fell into the way of "knocking off" by mutual consent at noon on days when they had to bake bread. If it was a little colder than usual in the morning they succumbed to the temptation of making more figures and dreaming more dreams by the fire and postponing work until the morrow. "The gold's in the ground; it's ours. All we've got to do is to take it out, and we've got to stay here two or three winters, anyway," was the argument with which they excused themselves. The size of their dumps beside those excavated by employees who worked by the hour was a silent commentary on the value of discipline.

Mid-July found them in Dawson in a mood

to afford at least one more dish of eggs, one more dinner at the restaurant before they settled down to the economical life which their necessities required. Occasionally they took out of their pockets, to amuse their friends, clippings from the home paper, in which they saw themselves made out millionnaires. They reread the letters from home which had come along with the clippings in the first mail down the river, and confronted deep perplexities. It was only human that they should wish that the wife had not gone so far as actually to order the piano and the gown. While they calculated how much they would need for their winter's outfit and how much they could send home— if that fund did not all go for eggs before the problem was settled — they formulated the wording of their replies by which they should explain the situation.

To the credit of the sex be it said that the wives of some of the unfortunate laymen knew their husbands' weaknesses. One optimist, who had taken only $900 out of his claim instead of the $10,000 that he had anticipated, received this reply from home:

"God bless you, Charlie, but we've made too many ten thousands without ever getting them for me to count my chickens before they're hatched. I'm being as economical as I can, and telling the neighbors that I hope you'll make a good year's wages, but that it's too early to tell yet for certain."

Most of the laymen, if they had worked steadily for eight hours a day—more are scarcely practicable on account of the long nights—would have had more than the equivalent of the prevailing rate of wages. Those who had felt themselves to be unfortunate in not getting lays and had sought employment, because they had someone to tell them to go to work in the morning, were in the mood of the school-boy who had studied during the term and passed his examination as opposed to the boy who had not. Their employers were better satisfied because their claims had been worked with more system and thoroughness than the others, and were more than glad to pay the interest, heavy as it was, on their borrowed capital.

While the laymen were inclined to exaggerate the amount of their earnings in order to decrease the discrepancy between their winter boasts and their spring returns, the claim-owners themselves, who early in May were serene optimists and put the total output of the country at $15,000,000, by the end of May were dour pessimists, asserting their unbounded faith that the total output would not be more than $6,000,000. Early in May, you see, there was an impression that the Government royalty of ten per cent. on the gross product of all claims had been repealed. At the end of May, Major Walsh, the Commissioner of the Yukon District, arrived with the positive information that the royalty would be collected. Most of the claim-owners on Bonanza had suffered the same disillusion as their laymen; but most of them, if the Government had not decided that they would have to pay the royalty on the laymen's gold as well as on their own, would have put on a bold front, especially as their claims were for sale.

When claim-owners met on the trail, after comparing notes as to the number of eggs eaten at the first sitting, the invariable remark was:

"I don't suppose you've heard anything about your claim being sold!"

For no one was certain whether he or some stranger owned the wealth of his dumps. Without any property under consideration by the capitalists of London or New York, you

A Flume on Bonanza Creek.

were a kind of social outcast. Claims that were under options were as common as mortgages formerly were on farms in Kansas.

The prospect of famine during the winter had been responsible for this. Some enterprising fellows, who were among the first to go out over the ice, made the best of their opportunity as connecting links between an isolated community and civilization.

"Here you are," they said to the claim-owners on Eldorado and Bonanza, "paying a dollar and a quarter and a dollar and a half an hour for labor and thawing the dirt out by inches, when capitalists, with cheaper labor and improved appliances, can take it out for half the money. Why, it's a case of the old stage coach against the lightning express. If they can block a number of claims and work 'em together, they'll gladly pay you on the spot more'n you can get out of your claim the way you're working it, and make a good thing out of it too. The whole outside's wild over the Klondyke. The capitalists are longing for the chance. All that's got to be done is to lay it before 'em. You name your price and give me six months' option and we'll take 'em out and sell 'em. What we get for 'em's our affair. We'll make our commission out of the difference."

The enthusiasts believed what they said. They assured themselves and the claim-owners that none of the arguments which held good in other mining camps could apply in this instance. The Klondyke was a law unto itself in all matters of investment, they said. They put dust from each of the claims which they were to sell in a separate bag, and this they were to offer to the simple-minded financiers of London and New York as a guarantee of the correctness of their several representations. Each zealous miner being desirous that his claim should show up well on the list, some of the promoters obtained several thousand dollars in nuggets.

Such examples of success were not without their effect upon those who went out over the ice at later periods. The field of all the claims on the creeks as yet demonstrated to be valuable having been worked, they turned their attention to those creeks which had been staked on unfounded rumors by stampedes, and possibly were worth no more than the beds of so many creeks in the valley of the Hudson River. They neglected none of the details. Because it looks better to the lay eye, they chose dust from Eldorado as examples of the product of these "wild oat prospectors."

The moral effect of the option craze was unfortunate in more respects than one. Men who owned claims on stampede creeks felt that they could afford to waste their winter in idleness in their cabins as long as they had property in the hands of New York capitalists. They could not escape the heresy that a claim in the Klondyke, no matter what its location, was regarded by the outside world as a valuable piece of property. It was especially hard for those who had not funds enough to buy their winter's outfit, as they inquired along the river bank, day after day, as the boats came in, to learn finally that the promoters to whom they had intrusted their claims had arrived on the Pacific Coast just at the time when the Klondyke was forgotten and all public interest was centred in another subject, and, accordingly, had enlisted in the volunteer army.

Those promoters with small ambitions fared the best. In London they sold a few of the cheaper claims, which, as a rule, were disappointments to the purchasers. But sometimes it is better to be trusting than to be wise. One young Englishman bought a claim on Sulphur for $2,000 which would not have sold for $500 in Dawson at the time. When he arrived to take possession of it in June, its value had risen so rapidly on account of the later development of the creek that he sold it for $20,000. The anxiety of the claim-owners on the new creeks, as Sulphur, Dominion, and Hunker—all having their head-waters on the slopes of The Dome—were called, lest the promoters had sold their claims, was as great as that of some of the claim-owners on Bonanza lest their claims had not been sold. Perhaps as many as thirty claims on the new creeks had been worked to any extent during the past winter, with such results as to increase their speculative value by five hundred per cent.

The forty happy kings of the forty claims on Eldorado also preferred not to sell. That "pup" returned good for evil. It heaped satire upon the satirists who had given it its name as a joke, and continued to surpass all expectations. The optimism which over-estimated Bonanza under-estimated Eldorado. These forty kings, as they compared the output with their figures, concluded, with some pride, that all born mathematicians are inclined to be too conservative.

You could see the dust glistening in the dumps of the " pup." The water gurgling over the cleats in the sluice-boxes seemed to sing a merrier song than on Bonanza. Every shovelful which it bore chuckling over the cleats yielded up a dollar or more. It licked twice as much off rocks that had to be lifted out of the sluice-boxes by hand because its current was not strong enough to carry them on down to the waste pile. At intervals, nuggets of some size were unearthed by the spade and were tossed into a pan at one side. If you were a friend of the claim-owner he would beg you to take your pick of the lot as a souvenir of the day. But you would not get one worth more than ten or fifteen dollars, even if you were greedy enough to choose it for its size rather than for its beauty. The giants—one was found worth $600 and those worth from $50 to $100 were not infrequent—had been spied in the drifts in the winter.

A magnificent carelessness of details prevailed. A scientific miner who had seen fortunes made in California out of a cent a pan would have regarded the forty kings in the light of infants making a holiday with a tack hammer and a gold watch. They could afford to laugh back at him in return. There is some reason in their philosophy that one cannot afford to pay men a dollar and a quarter an hour to pick up stray pennies, and more in the philosophy that when you have a fortune you have enough.

It was not yet in the old-timer's nature, rapidly as his character was changing, to squeeze the last cent out of Mother Earth, in the manner of some hard taskmaster, when she had given to him such a bountiful harvest. A little line of dust, like a braid of gold lace, remaining on either side of the sluice-boxes after a day's clean-up was dismissed with the remark that it would "come out in the wash" next time. If the workman who had the uncomfortable and unhealthy position—especially when the sun was directly overhead—of standing in the dump-box, took a few minutes' rest, he shrugged his shoulders and said that any dust that was lost in the meantime could be a boon to the Chinamen who, coming humbly after the white man's departure, would patiently take fortunes out of the white man's tailings—unless the capitalist should make the

Shovelling a Clean-Up into a Gold Pan.

Cleaning Up.

valley resound with the toil of machinery manned by cheap labor, thus cheating poor John out of what he has come to regard as the right of his race in placer mining countries.

There was not one strong box for the safe-keeping of the daily harvest of thousands on all of the creeks. The bags of dust were kept in the little cellars which the miners had excavated under their cabins for the preservation of their food. There was a joke which went the round of the firesides during the food-panic that it would be cheaper to fry the dust and save the hams. For the bags, made of roughly tanned moosehide, the Indians received prices in keeping with those of other things. They bore the owner's name printed in ink, if ink could be obtained; their capacity was about $5,000 each, and they were not unlike, in their freshness as well as in their size, the dirty, worn, brown little bags which were carried in lieu of purses. Three or four of them were all that you cared to carry on your back. When you met men on the trail bending as under heavy packs of slight bulk, you knew their business. If there were many bags there might be an escort with a rifle and there might not. Most of the claim-owners thought nothing of sending several thousands by their employees, unaccompanied, to be deposited in one of the Commercial Companies' stores ; but once the "Cheechawkos" began to arrive, all sought locks for their cellar-doors.

VI

SOME KLONDYKE TYPES

The Fool and his Lucky Friends—More Theorizers—Joe Staley and Billy Deddering — French Gulch Bench —Good Fortune that was Deserved—Neighbors and Twins—No Cure for the Gold Fever.

IT was the greater world of the Klondyke that was bounded by the creek claims. A smaller world was bounded by the hill-sides where there were many fresh mounds of earth, suggesting that the population might be digging their graves one by one. Graves of ambitions most of these mounds were, in all truth. A few, readily distinguished as far as you could see the two figures hovering over them, were the birthplaces of the fortune which the figures were exhuming with the orthodox rocker.

The original nugget washed out of a bench and deposited where Indian Charlie's gaze would light on it did not lead, even indirectly, to the discovery of the wealth of the benches.

IN THE KLONDYKE

This honor belongs to a stalwart Swede, whose race in the Klondyke is the general butt of that fine wit of our own race which makes a mark of a foreigner's broken English and his efforts to understand strange manners and a strange language. One day in the spring of 1897 he went up the slope above his cabin near the mouth of Eldorado and began to strip off the muck as fast as the sun thawed it. Directly his neighbors saw what he was doing they began to compose satirical remarks against the time when he should come down.

"Why don't you go looking for gold up a tree?" they asked him.

"I tank gold no grow on trees," he replied, in all candor.

"Say, did you ever hear," they continued, as they held their sides, "that the weight of gold makes it sink? I suppose you think the glacier walked up on the hills and left a few millions there. The millions didn't roll down? Oh, no! That's why we have to sink through thirty feet in the creek bed to pay dirt. Better try the trees! You might find a bear up the trees and bear meat would be worth three pennyweights a pound in town."

"If you don't dig some hole you no find

gold. By tam! I dig a hole if I vant to," he replied, as he went into his cabin.

"Well of all the fools," they said, "it takes a Swede to beat the lot."

Men passing on the trails stopped to look up to the point where the "fool" was working, grew friendly in despising him, and carried the joke to the ends of the creeks and to Dawson, where it was elaborated over the bars.

One evening the "fool" quietly called on all of his friends among his fellow Scandinavians, as well as upon certain Anglo-Saxons who had not made fun of his English. They followed him up the hill and drove stakes in the neighborhood of his prospect hole. The twinkle in his blue eye was not unkind, though suggestive, the next morning when he showed to the scoffers a handful of nuggets from a claim which was worth $50,000. But scoffers accept nothing on faith. They would not believe that he took the nugget out of the hill until they had panned some of his dirt themselves.

"Well, of all the lucky fools," they said, " it takes a Swede to beat the lot! Here's millions been lyin' within ten rods of us for a year and we never knowed it."

IN THE KLONDYKE

Those who had sharpened their wits at the discoverer's expense now hastened to get a claim as near as possible to his, until a mile of Bonanza on both sides of the creek was taken up, from the point where the slopes meet the creek bed to their summit. Theories about the habits of the glacier were qualified by the experts. Thenceforth, it stood to reason that the breadth of no glacier of such importance would be limited to that of a creek. The scoffers soon found themselves saying that this had been their opinion all along, and eventually became so imaginative as to hint that they had advised the Swede to make the experiment.

Poetic justice attended the immediate outcome of the stampede. The pioneer and the parasite got their fit rewards. There was less than an acre of good pay dirt on Skookum Bench, as it was called, and this mostly fell to the discoverer and his friends. Here and there in the neighborhood good day's wages could be made with a rocker, and nothing more. Enthusiasm over bench claims languished.

"It was just like a Swede to strike the only rich bench in the whole country the first time that he put his pick in the ground," said the scoffers. In their pessimistic philosophy, which exults over deserted prospect holes, the latest strike is always bound to be the last. They are the very ones who were the greatest optimists when they left home to try their luck in the North against the advice of their friends. This weakness is likely to grow on Klondykers who become too fond of a sedentary life, unless their supply of bacon runs out and forces action, or they awaken to a sense of their growing degradation when they eat fresh eggs in Dawson and then see the world in bright colors again. But long after the cynics are dead, strikes will be made in Alaska by the class of real prospectors who cheerily face all hardships and get out of them good digestions for anything from flapjacks to moose gristle or even boiled willow roots.

Joe Staley and Billy Deddering, who discovered French Gulch Bench, the richest of all the benches, the spring following the discovery of Skookum Bench, were of the order of real prospectors. They had served their apprenticeship in various parts of the Rockies, which are the playground of free men from end to end.

Fond as I am of the California prospector, I am unwilling to accept the verdict of his squint whenever he brings it to bear on a portion of the earth's surface, though Billy Deddering, I admit, as he understands relative values, has reason to believe in his. But, in one sense, I rejoice with him in his faith, inasmuch as the scoffers, who want to make out that all success in the Klondyke comes from luck, and that they have failed because they never had any, spun the yarn that a log which he was shooting down the hill for a cabin knocked a nugget out of the ground and thus became the godfather of his fortune.

Some two miles above the mouth of Eldorado, French Gulch splits the embankment which forms the western wall of the valley of Eldorado. Billy's squint, when he brought it to bear on the rounded corner of the embankment on the lower side of the gulch in something of the manner of an old-fashioned marine covering a sail with his telescope, told him that this was exactly the place where gold ought to be found, even if it was not. The first hole that he sunk yielded only colors. A clerk from London or the Eastern seaboard of the United States might have gone back down the hill with his pick and shovel in a fit of blues and never come up again. Billy was not in the least discouraged. He merely readjusted his squint, and concluded:

"If 'tain't here it must be farther up."

So it was. In the next hole he took $187 out of his first pan on bedrock. Joe was with him at the time, but at the request of Joe I give all the credit for the discovery to Billy.

"It was Billy's idea entirely," Joe said. "He spotted the ground first."

"What did you do," I asked Billy, "when you struck it after all your years of buffeting about from one camp to another?"

"Well," he replied, "I looked around to see if anybody had seen us."

"Nobody did see us, so far as we could make out," Joe put in, "but they must have noticed that we went down the hill as light as if we was walkin' on feathers, though we was tryin' to look very solemn, like we was at a funeral. When somebody asked us if we had found anything I reckon we kind o' started, though we was careful to say, 'Jest a few colors.' But durned if the crowd wasn't up there 'fore the few friends we had among our neighbors had fairly got their stakes in the ground."

"And you, Joe? What did you think of that night before you turned in?"

"Old's I am, and long's I've been knockin' about the world, I've never been married, and naturally I thought what a surprise it would be to mother, when she got a letter sayin' that her oldest boy was comin' back to 'hio with a pile to pay off the mortgage and spend the rest of his days on the old homestead."

"And you, Billy?"

"I wished I was in 'Frisco with that hundred and eighty-seven."

Many times I climbed the hill to have a talk with Joe and Billy. They were a relief from the loungers and speculators in the hotel at the Forks, who seemed to think that the business of a newspaper correspondent was to expound the possibility of the schemes for enlisting capital which they were promoting. It was a pleasure to look into the good faces of Joe and Billy, and to shake their hands, caked with clay. I sat on a stone and smoked my pipe, while Joe carried buckets of dirt to Billy, who looked up with a smile on his round German face, which was spattered with drops of mud that had splashed out of the rocker when he shook it, or when he ladled water on to the dirt with a dipper made out of a butter-can. Joe said that he didn't mind if the fact that he had struck it was published in the *Sydney* (Ohio) *Journal*, but beyond that I knew he had no axes to grind, and my highest ambition for the moment was that they should think me a good fellow, while their greatest fear was that I was starving because I would not go up to the tent and have a cup of coffee and a "bite to eat" in the middle of the afternoon.

The sun was accommodating enough to thaw the dirt as fast as Billy could rock it, and Joe could bring it a little faster than either the sun could thaw it or Billy could rock it. This allowed Joe intervals in which to rest, to entertain me, and to relight his pipe. I used to offer my pouch to him, telling him that he would get more smoke if he used tobacco.

"Couldn't think of it. There's nothin' so sweet as the heel," he would say. "It gives me a puff, and that's all I want."

It was not surprising that he wondered why the supplies of tobacco which other men had brought in with their outfits were long ago exhausted, while he had plenty left. He protested, notwithstanding Billy's denials, that he filled his pipe every morning—at least, almost every morning.

The experience of seeking with his own

hands wealth direct from the hands of Mother Nature had chiselled out the lines of his face in distinct, unqualified characteristics, without any of the doubtful gingerbread work which we find on faces in civilization. It was like the weather-beaten image on some old church, careless of the storms which make a new image streaked and mean. He and his "pardner" were "rocking out" five hundred dollars a day; he was no man's servant and no man's master, and more of a king than kings. I have gathered nuggets on his claim as easily as I have picked up white pebbles on the beach in boyhood.

The great difficulty is in developing such a wonderful squint as Billy Deddering's and in finding the exact spot where such nests of nuggets are located. If ever there was a poor man's claim it is the bench claim. All you need to work it are a rocker, which costs fifteen dollars, and your pick and shovel. A blind ditch whose frozen walls are as tight as a porcelain bath-tub will catch the seepage from the pay dirt, which is thawed by the sun as it is gradually exposed. So you have all the water that you need, without too much. If the bedrock be at some depth, you can work in winter as well as in summer. A year at the most will suffice to take out your fortune; and you have no worry over borrowed money, flumes, sluices, or dams.

If Billy had not already staked his bench claim rights for the Bonanza Creek region, he and Joe would not have had to be content with a single claim, and one of them would have got the claim just above discovered, which was even richer, two men taking as high as a thousand dollars a day out of it. Here was dirt richer than any on Eldorado itself, twenty of whose forty working claims, probably containing thirty million dollars, stretched out in a panorama before you when you looked either up or down the creek. If one could have had a claim on the bench of the size of the creek claims, instead of one only a hundred feet square, he would have been more than a millionnaire; and by hiring labor he could have left the country in three months after the discovery with his money in his pocket.

Sad to say, there was not room for all on French Gulch Bench any more than on Eldorado. The whole extent of the pay dirt was not more than two or three acres. It was just as large as the dip in the hill-side, which, according to the theory of Billy, caught and held the gold when it was travelling, while all that passed over the rim went on down to the creek bed below, leaving only an occasional color in its track. But I disagree with Billy. I think that all is accounted for by the giant keeper of the pot in The Dome having thrown out a handful of the overflow across the hills. This makes the presence of wash-gravel, which is absent, unnecessary, and reconciles itself to the presence of nuggets in rotten mica shist, which is the most inexcusable of all the paradoxes in Alaska, the old prospectors say.

Aside from Billy and Joe, I came to know some of their fortunate neighbors. Dan Saunders probably had the best claim of all. He was at the hotel at the Forks one day, and in his cups when a man offered in the bar-room to sell a claim on French Gulch Bench for a hundred dollars. The Forks is the Stock Exchange of the creeks, and at that moment, on account of some rumor, the opinion ruled that the bench had been salted. The claim-owner believed it. Dan said he would give fifty down and the first fifty out of the claim, and the offer was accepted. The morning after, when Dan's wit was not so brilliant, but his reasoning faculties had improved, he went up to look at his elephant. He came down a week later and tried to spend the two or three thousand dollars he had taken out in the meantime. He could dispose of only part of it, and returned to his claim in despair, somewhat disgusted with city life.

Burke, who owned the claim next to Saunders, was a type of the runaway boys from the East who have turned up in the Klondyke after having served an apprenticeship in the West. This one reaped among the harvest of his wild oats the largest nugget that was taken out of French Gulch Bench. It was the shape of an oblong pancake, without any quartz in it, and worth $210. When I met him in Dawson one morning, he was gleeful over the joke he had played on the old folks at home. For the first time in five years he had written to them. They had as good reasons to suppose that he was dead as that he was in the Klondyke.

"Won't their eyes pop and won't they have something to tell the neighbors when they find out that their worthless Tom is comin' home with fifty thousand cold!"

That same day I dined with Joe Staley at

the foremost restaurant in town. When we had eaten fresh eggs and other luxuries which had just been brought in from the " outside," as he pushed his plate away from him he shook his head dubiously :

"I dunno as I'll be so happy as I thought, when I settle down among the cows and chickens," he mused. "This grub don't taste the way I thought 'twould. Darned if I don't like the beans and bacon that I have up at the claim better, and I'll be glad to be back carryin' dirt to the rocker for Billy to-morrow. They say once the gold fever's in a fellow's bones it sticks like the rheumatiz, and I believe it. I reckon it's the only thing I'll be satisfied with in this life. But I won't prospect in this godless region. I'll go back to Californy."

On my way to see Joe and Billy I often stopped for a chat with Ned and Fred Beck, who were sinking a shaft to bedrock at the base of French Gulch Bench hill. These twin brothers had been "pardners" for forty years. They had the vigor which comes from living among the Rockies. Their faces, framed in white beards, were fresh and smiling. The archaic furnace which they had

The Discoverers of French Gulch Bench at Work.

Pardners and Twins for Forty Years.

constructed for sharpening their tools, if not their age and personal resemblance, would have attracted attention.

" Have you never quarrelled ? " I asked.

" Oh, yes, lots of times," said Fred, " and agreed on quits lots of times, too. After Ned's had a drink or two he always gets cranky and wants to start out for himself."

" Not much crankier'n you do," Ned put in.

" That's right," Fred assented. " But when we're sober we make it up again and are ashamed of ourselves. We may be twins, but we're just fitted for each other."

" That's right, too," Fred assented.

VII

GETTING ACQUAINTED

Mr. and Mrs. "Meenach" and their Menage—The Juvenile Mining Company, Limited—Voss—The Arch-Deacon—A Sour-Dough Stiff—A Dalmatian and a Turk—Siawash George and his Steam-engine—Miss Mulrooney at the Forks—The Price of a "Square" with Trimmings.

ONE day, if the quartz claims which have been staked should fulfil the hopes of their owners, the Klondyke will become a place of managers and workmen, of stamp mills and chemical processes. To-day, there is very little to say about the working of the mines, which is as simple as building a fire, digging a well and doing the week's wash, but much to say about my friends and acquaintances there, who came from the ends of the earth and represented most of its employments. Without knowing individuals, the pilgrimage of the Cheechawkos would have meant no more to me than a motley procession seen from a balcony. Those leading citizens and well-known characters whom I met, under the guidance of Captain Hansen in a round of the town on the evening after my arrival, are worthy of a chapter by themselves. If I had taken advantage of all the letters of introduction to claim-owners that they gave me I think that I should have been three weeks in travelling the length of Bonanza.

In return for hospitality that did not stand upon formality but laid its hand on my shoulder and insisted, I could offer nothing except the news from the "outside," the bad news that there was no escape from the royalty. I registered a vow that if I were to make the journey over the ice again I would find room among my supplies for one more article of luxury, or else forego the privilege of introductions. I saw in my dreams the smiles with which my hosts would have greeted the offer of a good cigar, until I had the conscience of a highway robber.

"Don't forget to call on Meenach!" said Captain Hansen. "He's the luckiest man in the country without exception. He doesn't have to darn his own socks and cook his own bacon and beans and you'll know him because he's sleek and fat and clean-shaven. I walk up the creek when I can get the time just for the privilege of poking my head in at Meenach's door. To a poor devil of a Klondyker it's a peep into paradise."

It was not enough that the fortunate Meenach should have his wife; he had also his little boy of six and his two little girls, one of four and the other of two years, with him. After he wrote to Mrs. Meenach that he had killed his lion, she came on to him; and she brought with her such thing as sheets, tablecloths, and pillows, and a regulation cookingstove. He never dared to compute just how much the stove had cost him, preferring not to have his enjoyment of the luxury allayed. The mere expense of bringing it up from Dawson would have bought two or three good ones at home.

To the miners the most wonderful feature of the Meenach cabin was the carpet on the floor. Some of them wanted to take off their boots before entering, and one suggested that if he were younger he would walk in on his hands.

"If you don't mind," he added, "I'll sit with my back to the sheets on the bed. It's too much at a time. I want to drift into this easy like."

"Folks who live in castles may be bothered by having too many rooms to care for," said Mrs. Meenach, "but not I, in my cabin. I could put the children to bed with one hand, stir something on the stove with the other, and set the table with the third, if I had it. It's no trouble to go to the market in the morning. All our fresh vegetables are in tin cans in the cache just outside the door. Oh, yes, there is much to be thankful for if I look at it in the right light. We kept our condensed cream, our canned asparagus and our canned peas all winter without being frozen. Then, please heaven, something green grows in this country. I have a little cranberry sauce from the poor cranberries on the hill-side, and I agree with the children that it is 'gooder'n' anything I ever tasted. If I could get a fresh cabbage I think I should eat it all without waiting to put salt on it. Now I live from day to day on the hopes of the eggs which are expected in on the first boats."

Thus she chatted while she warmed the tinned roast mutton in the frying-pan, boiled the evaporated potatoes and the tinned sweet corn.

"I'm not going to say that dinner, such as it

is, is ready," she said, "because, in the Klondyke, that is quite superfluous."

It is good when you have eaten beans for a month off a tin plate balanced upon your knee, to look upon a clean table-cloth again, to sit by the window of a cabin in blissful certainty that your journey is at an end, and have a good and gentle woman pour you a cup of tea. I remember the meal as a banquet, not a dinner. After it was over, the lord and master and I smoked our pipes until the little ones' heads began to nod, when I went into the cabin of one of his laymen to roll up in my blanket.

The children had reason to think that they were the only children in the world and to be as proud as princes. But Mrs. Meenach's fears lest they should be spoiled by the adulation of the miners were equally vain with her fears about their health. The extent of their illnesses was a day's indisposition on the part of the baby. Swathed in furs and scarfs until only their noses were visible and their limbs were as stiff as a doll baby's, they might go out to play with their sleds for a few moments at a time. Listening to the cries of the dog-drivers and the howls of their steeds, which had turned their mother's nerves on edge, had been as good as the kuh-chuk-chuk-chuk of a railroad locomotive to them. The miners, with frost-encrusted beards, were so many Father Christmases who rarely forgot to bring a present of a nugget when they came.

With the coming of spring, an old Californian took the baby in his arms while the brother and sister followed at his heels up the hill-side to his bench claim. He showed them to a log, where they sat very gravely while he unfolded to them a mighty scheme. In return for three kisses apiece, one to be delivered when the bargain was struck and two when the goods were delivered, he agreed to build for them a small rocker, so that they could start a Mining Company (Limited) on their own account.

Their dividends were large until one of the laymen found out that they were using the best portions of his dumps. Then the total income fell to a dollar a day, which the boy explained was due to laxness on the part of the president—his elder sister—and gross negligence on the part of the assistant manager—the baby—who insisted upon turning the gold pan bottom side up at critical moments. Their father played the part of the unskilled laborer, and sometimes when he was ordered to work he said, "In a minute!" an excuse which had to be accepted. The time came when the old Californian could no longer keep his joke to himself.

"Meenach, seems to me I 'member tellin' the youngsters that you'd carry water for 'em to work the rocker with," he chuckled.

It was by a diversion from my programme that I spent the next night with Voss. His name was not on my list, and I had never heard of it until I drifted into his cabin. I was attracted by his speech, which sounded a little unnatural in a community where expressions are intended to convey a meaning and not to subserve the rules of grammar. Despite his education, Voss was an old-timer among old-timers, greeting them all by their first names. The most ferocious of them, out of whose mouths an oath rolled with the ease and deliberation of their tobacco smoke, regarded him as a personal friend.

"He looks stuck up, but he ain't stuck up,' they said. "He's clean all the way down and all the way through and game as a grizzly bear, and we know. We've followed him on the trail."

GETTING ACQUAINTED

The sincere fellowship which he felt for them in return belongs to that philosophy which makes of the young men of old but impoverished families, good and cheerful prospectors, ranchers, and cowboys. Not in fancy—which misled so many poor souls among the Cheechawkos—but in fact, they prefer the independent life of a mining camp to working for a salary in a city; prefer washing their own dishes and rising at 3 A.M., and harnessing the dogs to start on the trail to going to an office every morning and leaving it every afternoon at a certain hour. By all the manners that stamp the man, Voss was a child of civilization, and such a child as was equal to carrying out his determination not to return to it until he was master in his own right of the little luxuries that keep the taste of ashes out of the mouth. Often he spoke of these, then ran his hands into the pockets of his overalls, took a pull at his pipe, and looked at his dumps with an anticipation as keen as that of some naval captain of Drake's day in sight of the chalk cliffs of England, after years in foreign countries on rations of hard biscuit.

"But even before I carry out my plans of travel," he said, "I shall buy a ranch, where I shall have a home with no other habitations in sight; where I shall have a good saddle-horse waiting for me, whenever I shall grow tired of town. Once you have become accustomed to the silence of the plains, the mountains, and the trail, mere country houses will not satisfy you —something gets into the blood."

"You all catch it, I see," I interrupted. "Joe Staley says it's like rheumatiz' and it gets not into the blood but into the bones."

"Yes, bones—blood and bones, both!" was the reply.

He had four retainers, who lived in his cabin: the boy, the Archdeacon, Jim, and Grouse, the fox-terrier. The boy was sixteen or seventeen. He had gone to the Klondyke, against his parents' wishes, to find himself nonplussed by the necessity of a food supply for the winter months. Voss put him on his feet. The Archdeacon was of the Established Church and a graduate of Oxford. He did not seem to be, but he must have been, older than the boy, for he was gray and the father of three children. Shortly after he was ordained archdeacon the something had "got into" his blood and bones, and he vacillated between the church and travel until his meanderings brought the promise of a brilliant career to the guardianship of a flock of Indians, halfway around the world. He baked the best bread that I ate in the Klondyke. Though he accepted praise on that score as quietly as he did everything else, I could see that it pleased him—better, perhaps, than the praise of a bishop. In getting breakfast, which he had taken upon himself as one of his tasks, his slippered feet moved about so softly that you were not awakened until his voice called you at the right moment.

"It is good to see many kinds of men and to do many things," he volunteered, as he lifted a flapjack from the skillet to my plate. "When all the world was going to the Klondyke, I had to join the throng. I got a lay on Bonanza and put some men to work on it. But, unfortunately, I had no food for myself. Mr. Voss"—the Archdeacon never omitted the Mister—"asked me to come and live with him through the winter. What a pity it is that there isn't such a good fellow as Mr. Voss to take care of every unfortunate fellow like me!"

Jim, in the language of the Klondyke, was a "sour-dough stiff," and he was certainly an unhappy man. A "sour-dough stiff" will, under no circumstances, eat baking-powder bread. This eccentricity, developed in the later years of a prospector's life, generates others which are its natural companions. He thinks that baking powder in the smallest quantity is poisonous, and, therefore, is as finicky and miserable as any other man who becomes a victim of dyspepsia through forever thinking of some means to avoid it.

In addressing his employer Jim uttered the word "Voss" in a harsh voice, as if calling attention to its nudity and implying that he would not subvert his rights as a free man by using "Mister," though he were to hang for it. He was the first to rise in the morning and he always prepared his own breakfast.

"Some folks don't like my cookin', an' I don't like some folks' cookin', either," he explained.

On some occasions, when he felt a little lazy, he would condescend to eat at the table with the others, but with an expression of martyrdom on his thin, old face. Voss told me that Jim would probably confide to me at the first opportunity how grossly the claim was mismanaged, and so he did. Voss forgave his eccentricities partly because they amused him and his friends, and partly because Jim was an expert in saving fine gold from floating down to the waste pile.

Jim's contempt for the Alaskan miner's knowledge of sluicing was pleasant to hear unless you had to hear it often. He had a miniature sluice for treating the residue which contains the lighter particles. It were better to step on the hem of your wife's skirt on the way to the theatre than to lay your hands on this fine gold machine, as he called it. Whether or not it was worth the time that Jim had spent in building it, was a grave question with Voss.

In making the "clean-up" Jim was the general in charge of the field. The best-natured men on the claim were selected to assist him, and even their patience sometimes gave out. Voss himself, accompanied by the fox-terrier, who was general superintendent of the claim, winter and summer, used to take up his station at the water gate. He did not always interpret Jim's orders satisfactorily, and I overheard this grumbling complaint:

"A man can't play with a dog an' pay 'tention to business at the same time."

Everybody about the claim except Jim was the slave of the fox-terrier's moods. In New

York or London you could have bought Grouse for five dollars. Voss was offered $200 for him by another claim owner, but would as soon have parted with his claim. I knew of only one other terrier in the Klondyke. He was a companion, deserving the affix of bull, of a doggy-looking man who walked up and down the river front of Dawson. He was usually limping on three legs, but not infrequently on two. He seemed to realize his position as the sole representative of civilized dogdom among thousands of savages, and he no more thought of surrender than a Roman prefect. The boast of his master that he could whip any two or three of the huskies was well founded. Even when he was attacked by a dozen he gave more wounds than he received, retreating with the dignity of one who belongs to a ruling race.

Provincial as Voss's claim was in its isolation from the world, its surroundings were cosmopolitan enough. Among his employees, aside from Germans, Swedes, and French-Canadians, were a Dalmatian and a Turk. The Turk was a good workman. When he had made his "stake" he was going to buy a fig orchard in southern California.

On the day that I visited the discovery claim

of Siawash George, which is only a short distance beyond Voss's, several Cheechawkos were panning some gravel at the very point where Indian Charlie had found the famous nugget. They did not wash out a single color, and passed on in disgust to do more prospecting on ground whose stakes—for the most part fallen down—had been driven so long ago that the weather had washed off the writing on their four hewn sides. Siawash George had expended several thousand dollars in buying and bringing an old boiler and engine up to his claim from Forty Mile. Owing to a fatal defect in its pumping gear it would not supply half a sluice-head of water or do the work of a small dam; but the noise of its puffing and his ability to hire an engineer to superintend it at $15 a day greatly amused a mind which had become aboriginal from family associations.

Money playing an important part in the politics of Alaska as well as in other countries, poor George had acquired a fortune only to find that it was two-edged and might be an obstacle, as well as instrumental, in the fulfilment of his royal ambition. On a fatal day he had brought from Dawson to his wife some little brown things in a box which was lettered in gilt. She had found them so superior to plain brown sugar that they had opened a new world to her. She gave over her rights to a throne to dream of the day when she should take passage on a Yukon steamer to the land where shops were filled with chocolate bonbons.

Joe Powers was a near neighbor of Siawash George. As both had squaw wives there was a bond of union between them, and they visited back and forth a great deal. Joe could not read or write, I was told, but his good fellowship shone out of his ever-grinning face.

"Some of the boys I knowed down in Circle and Forty Mile that's struck it big," he told me in confidence, "is going into s'ciety when they get on the outside. But I ain't. How I would look in s'ciety, wouldn't I? The rest of the boys are about on the same pattern, too, I guess, only they can't see it when they look into a pool of water. I'm thankful I know them dodgers on the outside are too clever for me. I'll buy a fruit farm in Californy. Nobody can beat me out o' that."

However dangerous a little learning may be to some of the old-timers, one does not envy them their dust, spend it how they will. It is fitting that they who bore the brunt of the robust business of pioneering should occupy the cabins of the masters on the Eldorado and the Bonanza claims. Graduates of colleges and universities, who work for them with pick and shovel for a dollar an hour, arrived on the scene after the great strikes, and must take the consequences.

It is scarcely half a mile from Siawash George's to the cluster of cabins at the mouth of Eldorado; and Eldorado flows into Bonanza about midway of its working claims, making of The Forks, as the confluence of the two streams is called, the hub of a wheel with three spokes. When Miss Mulrooney came up to The Forks in the autumn of 1897 she appreciated the mathematical advantage of the situation at once, and acted upon her perception with such decision that the news of her wonderful undertaking went up and down the creeks that very day.

"Boys," said the heralds to the scoffers, "there's a new woman up to The Forks with a bit of an Irish brogue and the tongue of a lawyer, that's goin' to show us old moss-backs how to get rich. Hanged if she ain't got so much money to lose that she's goin' to build a two-story hotel bigger'n any in Dawson right up here on the creeks."

"Strange things was to be expected from the Cheechawkos once the news of a strike got into the newspapers all over the States," said the scoffers; while the saloon-keepers, being specialists on the subject, apprehended with professional disdain that Miss Mulrooney might as well start a hotel at the head of the Stewart or at the North Pole.

The next instalment of news related that Miss Mulrooney was up on the hill-side superintending the labors of the one lone mule surviving of those brought down the river on rafts in the summer, which she had hired for $20 a day to drag logs to the site of her building. That class of women who are too common in the Klondyke are not given to this sort of thing; and, moreover, they wear bloomers, while Miss Mulrooney wore long skirts. A new woman deserved punishment for such folly, but a good woman who wore long skirts was entitled to the friendly advice which one of the leading claim-owners undertook to supply.

"I've been in the country some time," he told Miss Mulrooney, "and I don't mind tell-

Miss Mulrooney of The Forks.

ing you for your own interest that Dawson's the place, not The Forks, for a hotel."

"Now, that's kind of you," assented Miss Mulrooney. "And may I ask if you would like something to drink?"

"Er-r-r, well," stuttered the Committee of One, as he tried to get his bearings, "well, I admit I sometimes do, like the most of the boys—but I didn't know as you'd be mentionin' that."

"Oh, I'm not, and I'm not likely to," with a toss of her head, "when I know there's no chance of your accepting. Of course, if you or any of the other boys was hungry or thirsty you wouldn't think of buying a drink or a meal up here. You'd walk sixteen miles to Dawson and back for it, wouldn't you? And the boys going over the divide to Dominion or Sulphur when they break the journey at The Forks would hang up in a tree over night before they'd sleep in a hotel, wouldn't they, now?"

A light burst upon the Committee of One.

"You'll pass, Miss Mulrooney, you'll pass," he said. "You kin take care o' yourself all right. With that head of yours, you'll own the Klondyke by the time you've been in the country as long as I have."

And the word that Miss Mulrooney was all right was passed along the line. Every man on the creeks looked forward to the date of the opening of her hotel. A democratic community could not confer titles, but it might call her Miss Mulrooney of the Forks, and thus she will be known for all time among Klondykers.

Meanwhile, she expected that every day would be the lone mule's last. There was neither hay nor oats in the country. As the story was told to me, he held body and soul together on birch bark and willow sprouts until the final log was dragged to the foundations, and then promptly expired.

"He had nothing to live on," as Miss Mulrooney expressed it, "and nothing to live for, and I'm thinkin' the poor fellow was so slow because he just knew that his interest in the enterprise was all that kept him up; and, like the rest of us, he wanted to postpone the last hour as long as he could."

The third night after the hotel was opened the Committee of One, himself, had to sleep on the floor because the bunks were all taken. Nothing could have served Miss Mulrooney better than the food-panic of midwinter. She had bought a full supply before everyone be-

A Yukon Steamer.

gan to hoard whatever beans or flour or whiskey he could get. All but two of the restaurants in Dawson had to close their doors. The two exceptions on fête days gave butter and apple sauce along with bacon, beans, and coffee. Their owners grew to regard Miss Mulrooney as their animate consciences whose voice was that of every miner who ate a meal in Dawson when he was down from the creeks.

"I don't mind paying double," said the Committee of One, to a Dawson waiter, "s'long 's I get suthin to eat. Just bring that dinner over again. Then I'll have only half a square meal for $5, not to mention that no fixin's go with it. Miss Mulrooney charges $3.50 for a square, but she gives you canned beef, canned mutton, and ham, and fixin's, and keeps askin' you if you won't have more and you keep acceptin' till you have to send for a drink 'fore you're strong enough to get up from the table. Jumpin' John Rogers! How you fellers must suffer when you pass out a bean and a rind and think of what a woman is doin' up there to The Forks!"

If you want to reach a man's heart through his stomach in a scurvy-stricken country, feed him, if it is the best you have, with sauce made of dried apples. Miss Mulrooney kept a great bowlful of this on her table. The transient ate of its contents with the ravenousness of the thirsty traveller drinking from a spring of cold water. No sooner was it emptied—I know by actual observation of a quart of apple-sauce having been eaten by two persons—than it was filled again by the cook, rapid if rough in his movements, who picked it up and put it down as if it were a red-hot ingot.

The ground floor of the hotel was divided into the bar-room and the dining-room. Cards were permitted, but no gaming-tables were maintained. Upstairs was a tier of bunks running along the wall, with a passageway between them. The blankets seemed cleaner than elsewhere—no hotel had sheets—and the bunks had curtains. Either a nice sense of individuality or sheer fatigue restrained the guests from removing their socks, and I have known miners who were over-tired by a long tramp not to remove their boots. They had enough respect for Miss Mulrooney to hang the soles of them over the edge of the bunk, however, though, if in their dreams they should participate in a stampede to some new creek, their good intentions were sadly belied. The

GETTING ACQUAINTED

sole occupant of a lower bunk, which was supposed to accommodate two in case of necessity, might be awakened at any hour by a nudge, and :

"Pardner, sorry to trouble you, but I guess you'll have to move over a bit to make room for me."

In winter the curse of a Klondyke cabin, banked with snow, chinked with moss and dirt to the last crack and knothole, is lack of ventilation. In summer, when there is no night and no two men quite agree on their hours of sleep or hours for travelling, it was as good as reading a local newspaper to try to sleep at Miss Mulrooney's. The widening cracks between boards of fir (put into the floors and partitions while yet green) never permitted the slightest details of conversation over the card-table or over the bar to be inaudible, except during unavoidable and scarcely welcome intervals when you heard the tramping and scuffling of heavy boots. I could discern the direction the traveller was going upon entering the dining-room door ; whether he was coming up stairs to bed, or was going to call out to the cook for a "squar" or "half a dozen eggs."

Andrew, a quiet, soft-voiced, obliging young man, who wore a white shirt and was solicitous about keeping his tie straight, had charge of the bar. According to all the traditions of new placer mining camps he was as much out of place as the average bartender would be in a chair of moral philosophy. He was so essentially lacking in combativeness that no one ever thought of picking a quarrel with him. Luck and whiskey, however, despite the Northwest Mounted Police, will generate in miners a surplus energy which they are inclined to expend upon furniture if not upon one another. Miss Mulrooney did not depend for purposes of pacification upon a huge St. Bernard who was always at her side when he was not drawing her upon her sled up and down the creeks in winter, but rather upon her blarney. She knew when, where, and just how much to apply.

"I always appeal to their best instincts," she said. "It's easy to lead and hard to drive. That's what you men don't understand. You try to drive."

I saw her theory put to the test of practice. A giant who was so well on in his cups that he could scarcely walk, concluded, only half an hour after he had finished one, that he wanted another meal. When it was placed before him he seemed to think that the cook was trying to hurt his feelings by making him eat twice, and with an oath he threw a dish of stew on the floor. Miss Mulrooney happened to be passing through the room at the time. She stepped over to him and told him in her pleasantest tone that accidents would happen.

" Accident ? " he asked, dazedly.

" Of course," she said. " I know you're too much of a gentleman to do such a thing purposely."

" Coursh ! Coursh it was ! " he kept repeating, as he dropped down on to his knees and tried to scrape the stew up into a little pile, despite her protests.

Then out of the maze of his crippled memory another horror presented itself suddenly and prompted him to arise.

" Miss Mulrooney," he asked, his face very red, " did you hear me swear ? "

" A little one—a slip," she replied.

He told her that it was only a real lady who would put so liberal a construction on what he called a breach of " ettykit." Fearful, nevertheless, that she might secretly think ill of him, he followed her about the hotel with apologies and dripping hands while he kept repeating how a poor devil might be a little weak, so rarely did a good bench claim fall to a poor devil's lot, until the inner workings of his conscience culminated in a full confession that the plate had not been broken by accident but intentionally. She forgave him even this, and then he went up-stairs and to sleep.

"What I want to do is to make money, you may be sure," Miss Mulrooney would say if you persuaded her to tell you her story. "I was born in Scranton, Pennsylvania. I had to earn my own living before I was out of short skirts, and I kept on doing a little better from one thing to another, till I was stewardess of a steamer on the Pacific Coast. There's nothing like being a stewardess to develop your wits when you're just a bit too independent for the job and you have to give the passengers as good as they send when they're sassy. I remember an old Englishman who expected me to black his boots. I told him I wouldn't, and I told him if he put 'em outside his door again I'd be thinkin' he was wantin' ice-water and turn a pitcherful into 'em. He went to the captain. The captain was a Scotchman and he didn't believe in puttin' on airs; and when the captain sent for me and I went to the captain's room I found the old gentleman there. Before we came out I had him laughin', and I'd never blacked his boots, either. But runnin' errands doesn't suit me. I started for the Klondyke as soon as I heard of it, and like the rest I'm going back either rich or broke."

The last time I saw Miss Mulrooney she was in Dawson searching for a good location for a hotel which was to have sheets and be positively palatial. Three weeks later, so I am told, it was completed. Once her first venture succeeded, she had begun to speculate in mining properties. Her position at The Forks gave her exceptional opportunities for inside information, and she was a "pardner" of a dozen leading citizens in as many enterprises.

"If you ever go to Chicago or New York," I suggested to her, "the women's clubs will be making a heroine of you as an example of what their sex can do."

"Not if I know it," she replied. "They won't, I'm thinkin', if they hear I sold whiskey. Besides, there's nothin' new about me. I'm old-fashioned."

IN THE KLONDYKE

Without abusing a much-abused word, I think that Miss Mulrooney may be called a remarkable woman, more particularly as her own opinion of herself is quite the contrary.

VIII

ARCTIC TRAITS

DAILY LIFE IN DAWSON—RENTING A CABIN—CIRCUMVENTING THE HUSKIES—JOEY BOUREAU AND HIS RESTAURANT—THE FARO DEALER'S WIFE AND HER BAKERY—THE LAUNDRYMAN AND HIS CLAIM—JACK BELTZ'S SCHEMES—A PAIR OF DREAMERS.

IT depends upon the season of the year whether the town-site of Dawson is liquid, mushy, or as flinty as frozen ground can be. At one time in the summer of 1898 most of it was under water. Two weeks later, the Yukon having fallen some sixteen feet, this same town-site was at a respectable height above the level of the stream. The smaller sandbar on the opposite side of the mouth of the Klondyke, which, out of respect to the cabins which cover an area of six or seven acres, has been called Klondyke City, is without the surface layer of muck which held sewage as in a sponge under the noses of the residents of Dawson. The good nature of the fellow, known as "Dud," who keeps the sole saloon and hotel at Klondyke City, was as largely responsible for our choice of abode as the healthfulness of the location. Empty cabins were scarce. "Dud" said he had one to rent. When I asked him the price, I offended him.

"You walk right in and stay till I tell you to get out," he said. "But if you go shakin' your dust in my face I won't let you have it at all."

So we stood our sleds up beside the door, set up our little Yukon stove, threw our blankets on the floor, and were at home. The comfort of my daily existence I felt to be great compared with a bunk in a bunk-house for $2.50 a night, or a room with cloth partitions over a bar for $10 a night.

Fritz, who liked movement and life, went over to town to live in the cabin of a friend, leaving Jack and me to do our own cooking or to eat at the restaurant when we were of idle mind. The dogs also patronized the restaurant without standing on ceremony. "Jack" carried off almost the last ham in the camp, having lifted it from a nail with the unostentatiousness of an expert thief. The proprietors of the restaurant would not listen to reimbursement. They explained that anybody who had been in the country for six years and let a husky dog get the better of him deserved to be mulcted. It is out of deference to the husky dog that the miner builds little caches, set on poles, for storing food, which make the town look like a Bornese village, whose inhabitants have deserted their old homes to live in cabins.

The proprietors of the restaurant, in my opinion, were well worth knowing. Joey Boureau—undeniably French-Canadian, but forever repeating that he was a citizen of the United States—was almost as dark as a Moor, with the torso of a Turkish wrestler. He yielded neither to excess nor fatigue, blustered at times, never cared for to-morrow, and was possessed of a ready wit. His blague had a counterpart in the blarney of his partner, Tim, undeniably Irish American and proud of it. This pair had been inseparable for the many years that they had sought gold with the pick and in all the ways of camp life. Upon the scales at the end of the oilcloth-covered dining table they weighed out $2.50 worth of dust out of your bag whenever you ate off their board. Whichever one happened to be in did the cooking, and if both were in, one told stories to amuse the guests and acted as cashier.

But both were seldom there. One was usually at "Dud's" faro table. The other, when he grew tired of working brought his "pardner" home on his arm, installed him in the kitchen, and immediately went out to enjoy a little recreation on his own account. As he took with him whatever dust there was in the tomato-can, which served as their cash-box, we heard frequent excuses for the absence of moose steak on the table because of lack of funds to purchase it. Just as their business was beginning to prosper they sold it for a song to a Cheechawko whom they met on the river-front. A week in town sufficed to spend the song, and then they put packs on their backs and started over the hills, whistling as they went.

In one of the neighboring cabins the wife of a faro dealer had set up a bakery. We paid her fifty cents apiece for pies and fifty cents for loaves of bread, and had to order them beforehand to make sure of getting them.

Our laundryman had staked a claim in which he placed great hopes; but his invariable charge remained seventy-five cents a garment. He related with a realism almost tragic the details of the processes by which he had arrived at the original color of the khaki trousers that I had worn on the trail. Jack Beltz, for his part, se-

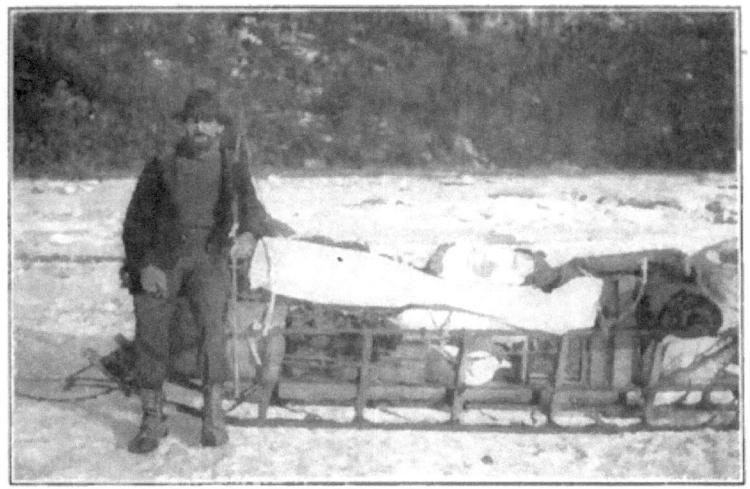

Jack Beltz.

"The Huskies."

cured the loan of an old tub and a washboard, and after a day's labor surveyed bandanna handkerchiefs and what not hung out on the line with the mien of a conqueror.

Economy, however, was always a matter of necessity with him. On the first night of his return from town he said, with some pride, that he still had most of the dust which he had received in conclusion of our contract. The next night before going to bed he built a fire in the stove out of the driftwood which he snaked out of the river for fuel, and sat for a long time in a reverie.

"Well, I'll have to earn some more," he said, finally, to himself, and dropped upon his blankets.

In the morning, followed by his troop of dogs, who had regained their spirits and their flesh, because he had fed them so bountifully, he went up on the mountain side, where he picked a great bouquet of the wild flowers which spring up in such profusion in summer. He never told me of his losses, and I tried to avoid the appearance of suspecting the truth, at the same time that I took practical measures to obviate an effort to dispose of his robe for cash and to hypothecate his year's outfit, which was to be brought down the river by his "pardner," Cliff.

Meanwhile, he revolved in his mind many schemes for making money. The price of moose steak, $1.50 a pound, suggested to him that a fortune might be made in moose hunting. Learning that Dawson had no bowling alley, he so far arranged to start one as to find that balls and pins could not be obtained nearer than Seattle. This scheme was succeeded by the more alluring prospect of taking dogs, which are valueless in summer, as they are valuable in winter, to an island in the river to feed for so much a month. Always before his dream had taken definite form he dismissed it by saying he was no city man. He recalled his experience in keeping the restaurant in a British Columbia mining town, and he reverted to a proposition that was to the liking of his love of robust vagabondage :

" I'll get a pardner and take the dogs and go up to the head-waters of the Porcupine and cross over to the Mackenzie. It would be a rattling trip ! "

As if in excuse of his venture he would add that he was certain to find gold in that region.

One day another dreamer, Kidd, came to

join us. He was a protégé of Jack, who had found him trying to put his outfit over the Pass. There must have been such giants as Kidd, with such straight noses, curling black hair and curling black beard, in the phalanxes that confounded the Persians. But this type of the freshness and strength of country life was quite modern. He slouched into the cabin with his hands in his pockets, and included in the drawl with which he greeted us a Missourian "Doggone it!" Like many other unfortunate fellows, Kidd had been obliged to spend the whole winter in the neighborhood of the Pass. Jack and his partner had made him a tent-mate in their camp on the banks of Linderman, during the dreary period of waiting. Going on to Le Barge after our departure from Linderman, he had arrived in Dawson before Cliff.

"That boy comes from a good family," said Jack; "and I'll bet they're proud as anybody that ever had a grand-dad who owned a lot of niggers and went stone broke after the war. He don't say nothin' about it, but it sticks out all over him. He didn't know how to hitch a pack on a mule's back when I first met him. But though he was green, he wasn't fresh; and when tenderfeet are that way they'll learn and you like to learn 'em. When they ain't, you like nothin' better than to give 'em the worst bronch' on the ranch and leave 'em to find out things for themselves."

It was not until after considerable urging that Kidd would consent to share our cabin. His character was in sharp contrast to that of another young stranger who entered and threw his blankets on the floor for the night without any formalities. In the morning, picking up certain articles of my kit which were lying beside my bed, he said:

"You're goin' out on the first steamer. Don't suppose you want these, do you? I'll take 'em along. They'll come in handy next winter."

"He'll get on," quoth Jack, "but I'm ding-donged if he'll get on with my help."

Jack now included Kidd in his schemes, which became more and more attenuated. Kidd would walk back and forth for some time as if in deep thought, and finally drawl:

"Gee-mo-nee! We must do something, Jack!"

And Jack, as he looked out upon the rapidly flowing river, would agree, and relight his pipe.

Kidd admitted that he was homesick, "dog-goned homesick." He had a right to be, for he left home with a thousand dollars and his mother's blessing, instead of finishing his education and studying for the country bar.

"Gee-mo-nee!" he exclaimed. "I was green, wasn't I, Jack? I thought you'd just pick the gold up once you got here. But doggoned if I'll go back broke. I'll have as much as I had when I left or stay forever. I've got three hundred of that thousand and I'll make seven hundred and my fare out some way this winter."

One day the dreamers found employment on the log booms for the new saw-mill that was to be built on the island in the Klondyke between Dawson and Klondyke City. Jack was as much at home on a rolling log as on the back of a broncho. Poor Kidd fell into the water often, but showed great persistence until the rise in the river made work impossible and left them idle again. So Jack sat by the cabin door keeping a lookout for Cliff, the third giant of the trio, who arrived one day, with a broad grin.

"Gosh!" he exclaimed, as he grasped Jack's hand. "I was washed out of the boat when we came through Five Finger Rapids, and blamed if I wasn't washed in again! How's that for luck?"

There was something of the New England Yankee in him, though he had been born in Colorado.

"I'll bet you've give your money all away, ain't you, Jack?" was his next remark. "You wouldn't be Jack if you hadn't."

"Weeks ago," was the reply.

They secured a contract with one of the saw-mills to cut rafts of logs sixty miles up the river. Here was a chance for Jack to swing an axe, to build bonfires, and to do what he called an honest man's work. With his dogs around him on the day of his departure I said a regretful good-by to the vagabond.

IX

PILGRIMS' TRAILS AND TRIALS

Itineraries—Alleged Unimportance of Experience—The Case of Father Stanley—Press Agents and Primers of Wealth—The Secretary of the Seattle Chamber of Commerce His own Convert—Pardners and Promoters—Outfits—Home Comforts for an Arctic Climate—Heterogeneous Boat Loads—The Nancy G—Tragedies of the Passes.

NEXT to taking part in some event chronicled on the bulletin boards your average pilgrim of fortune best enjoyed being near them. Least of all he liked waiting in latitude 64 degrees for a month or more for news of progress of the only war yet waged by his country in his generation. When he left home the Klondyke was the ruling general topic of the hour in the newspapers. When he reached his destination he was quite forgotten, and public interest was entirely absorbed in the invasion of Cuba.

Viewed in one light, there was good reason for the pique which he naturally felt toward

Shafter's army. He might see many wars, for instance, before he saw the like of this Dawson pilgrimage again. Thirty-five thousand generals, each one his own quartermaster, packing a thousand pounds of food apiece over a rugged coast range of mountains, building a flotilla with axe and whipsaw out of the primeval forest, and travelling six hundred miles into a country having an arctic climate in winter and a tropical climate in summer and yielding no food except a little game, presented a spectacle more romantic, if not so exciting, as the massing of an army corps under one general, its extension into a battle line, and the capture of the enemy's outposts.

The old prospector from California, British Columbia, Australia, or South Africa formed only a small percentage of those who entered, with the enthusiasm of children, a world of effort quite new to them. The village loafer and the ne'er-do-well son of the banker became partners on the trail. Mechanics who had mortgaged homes bought with savings from their wages to buy an outfit, rubbed elbows with broken-down speculators and business men who hoped to recover all that they had lost by finding a placer mine. The farmer, the clerk, the

On the Pass.

artisan, and the city or the provincial day laborer of the Eastern States, Eastern Canada, and England, were as confident of success as their associates who had learned in the severe school of the plains, the veldt, or the bush how to preserve life and health in a new country. If they had not swung a lariat or a pioneer's axe, they had at least beaten someone in walking or rowing or had gone longer without eating than any of their immediate friends.

Of the eighty thousand who left their homes for the Klondyke in the winter of 1897–98 and the spring of 1898, some thirty-five thousand arrived at Dawson. The battle was not always to the strong. More important than physical strength were determination and cheerfulness. Those who failed were as peculiarly Anglo-Saxon as those who succeeded; for they had the restlessness which impels one to seek obstacles but does not necessarily provide the force to overcome them. Most of those who had endeavored to reach Dawson in the autumn of 1897 were stranded on one side or the other of the passes, where they had to wait through a dreary winter until the ice which had arrested their progress should go out of the river. But only a small proportion of the whole number of pilgrims made this attempt. The great majority planned to transport their outfits over the passes in the early months of 1898 and build their boats on Lakes Linderman and Bennett in the interval between good travelling in a snow-bound country and the opening of navigation.

All pilgrims, whatsoever their itineraries, were grist for the mills of the towns of the Pacific Coast States and of British Columbia, bringing welcome relief from a period of commercial depression. Enterprising merchants, chambers of commerce, and steamship companies scattered broadcast throughout the United States (whence came seventy per cent. of the pilgrimage, ninety per cent. of it being Anglo-Saxon) pamphlets, well written for the purpose, telling " How to Get to the Klondyke."

The career of " Father " Stanley, of Seattle, was used as a stock illustration of the unimportance of experience to the prospector. This lame old bookseller, having the enthusiasm of the fanatic in place of real strength, had gone to the Klondyke in the spring of 1896. For a time he worked on the bars of Stewart, taking out $10 a day. If he had not been deformed he would have packed more food over the Pass. Fortunately, his supply ran out in September, and on his way down stream to Forty Mile, where he hoped to get more, he happened to arrive at the mouth of the Klondyke just as the first miners from Forty Mile were hurrying to the scene of Indian Charlie's " strike." As he could not walk as fast as the others, they got all the claims on Bonanza, and he had the good luck to get one of the best claims on Eldorado.

A year later, returning on the treasure ship that brought the news of the great strike, when he entered his house with a small portion of his fortune—a hundred thousand dollars in cash—his good wife, as the story goes, was at the washboard, where she had spent a deal of her time during her husband's absence, earning a living for a large family. Her customers coming to make inquiries about their clothes were told to take whatever was in the tub which they could identify as their own. As for herself, she was boarding at the hotel, sending such of her apparel as she had not thrown away to the laundry, and, moreover, was too busy with the dressmaker to attend to any trifling details which might have concerned her past life.

"In the frozen fastnesses of the far North fortunes nestle in nuggets of glittering gold for all"—but the press agents were too well versed in human nature to say that these fortunes were to be had for a pleasure trip. They mentioned hardships which put up a price of success, thus making the nuggets more attractive, and, in a sense, supporting the assertion of their existence. Anyone who would overcome the hardships might have a competency for the trouble of thawing it out of the frozen ground. No pilgrim felt himself to be less courageous and vigorous than "Father" Stanley; and the wives of all pilgrims were equally certain that, under similar circumstances, they could conduct themselves with quite as much dignity as Mrs. Stanley.

As became a primer to wealth, the pamphlets told just how much it would cost to reach Dawson with the all-necessary year's outfit, going to the trouble, in a spirit of solicitude and rectitude, of setting down opposite each article of food and each utensil, whether spade or gold-pan, or oakum or pitch, or nails for boat-building, its cost in dollars and cents, and adding up a fascinatingly small total from a very tall column of figures. With a receipted bill for this, and having paid his fare to Dyea or Skaguay, where he would disembark on the mainland of Alaska and begin the transportation of his outfit over the passes, the pilgrim, although he was supposed to have expended only $300, needed no more money to take him to his mine.

It was not to the credit of the calculations of the pamphlets, and not testimony, in all if it was in some instances, to the success of the numerous gambling establishments that sprang up at the point of mobilization of the army of fortune-seekers, that the Seattle post-office did an overwhelming business in money-orders in December, 1897, and January and February, 1898. The authors of the pamphlets were not called to account for their errors. Rather, they received the thanks of their employers. Once he was on the coast, it stood to reason that while he was yet sleeping between sheets and eating meals cooked by someone other than himself the pilgrim would not retreat because he needed a few more dollars which were obtainable from friends or relatives at home.

Seattle's success beyond all other towns in attracting trade was due to a university graduate and an author of works on art. Having to give up journalism in the East and seek health in the West, after some severe tests of versatility of earning a living, he became Secretary of the Seattle Chamber of Commerce. Such were the results of his knowledge of the peculiarities of the Easterner, the Westerner, the Canadian, and the Englishman, which he incorporated in separate pamphlets, that his employers continued to raise his salary from week to week until the war broke out and he relieved them of the embarrassing consequences of their transports of generosity by resigning and starting for the Klondyke himself (regardless of his doctor's advice) as a convert of his own arguments.

The camp-followers of the host of individual quartermasters which Seattle equipped and embarked, besides the gambler and the pickpocket, included many men of elastic consciences and elastic schemes, who had no capital but were ambitious to become capitalists. Those promising large dividends on properties yet to be purchased or staked were common; those proposing such grand things as running snow and ice locomotives over the hummocks of the Yukon in winter were in some measure distinguished. In the corridors of the crowded hotels you overheard the consultations of "pardners" as well as the harangues of promoters.

Sacks of flour, bacon, and beans, the chief constituents of the Yukon outfit, were piled on the sidewalks. In the windows of the stores were samples of various improved edibles and home comforts for an arctic climate. Fakirs on the curbs proclaimed the merits of patent sleds, portable boats, and devices for thawing frozen ground. In selecting his outfit, the pilgrim experienced the same emotion as the young wife who furnishes a flat. When he had settled on the kind of sled, the kind of stove, and the kind of tent that he was going to take, he faced the important question of buying dogs or of drawing his own supplies from Dyea or Skaguay to the lakes. If he had money enough he usually fell a victim to the speculators, who sold the house dogs that they had shipped into Seattle, after a few days' training in harness, for fifty dollars apiece.

The last article of his outfit bought, he waited for his steamer to sail, while his hotel bill grew apace. Liberal navigation laws, at all times carelessly enforced, in these piping times of prosperity became a dead letter. Every available sailing and steam craft in the Pacific marine, which is comparatively small and is largely recruited from the Atlantic seaboard, was called into service by the demands of the pilgrimage. Fortunes were made in two or three trips of vessels, which had been condemned as unseaworthy years before. To get all the passengers they could carry they had only to offer transportation for a pilgrim and a ton of supplies at a little less exorbitant price than any of their rivals.

Inexperienced pilots steered many vessels on to rocks in the tortuous and narrow channels between the barren and mountainous islands of the Alexander Archipelago which skirt the coast of British Columbia and the adjoining territory of southeastern Alaska. Pilgrims not yet embarked were too anxious about their own departure to think of the miseries of those who had suffered from exposure and lost their outfits, if not their iives. Rarely did the best steamers leave within less than a week of their appointed sailing time. In loading them there was little discrimination or even classification. Quarters of beef for the restaurants of Dyea and Skaguay, dogs in crates and in leash, mules and bales of hay, were put on the decks after

Caches of Pilgrims' Outfits at the Summit.

the hold was filled. Considering the experiences of a volunteer army with a single quartermaster, better things were scarcely to be expected of a volunteer army composed entirely of quartermasters. The chaos had the sole attraction of not bearing the stamp of officialdom.

As an example of what a pilgrim might suffer, there was the case of the Nancy G. When I left Seattle on February 15th, on the Nancy G.'s mast still fluttered the torn ends of a cloth sign with fast-fading red letters: "This fine schooner in the tow of a powerful ocean tug, will positively sail for Dyea on January 25th." Every day the passengers went down to the pier to see if their outfits were still on board and to see how repairs were getting on. A man with a hammer in one hand and some oakum in the other came out of the hold.

"You needn't cuss me," he said. "A schooner that's been resurrected after five years in the graveyard, ain't what she was when she was new, and you oughter know it. Every minute I lose caulkin' up the old girl's corn out of your own crops."

Afterward they went to see the owner, who received their complaints with an air of disdain, refused to return the amount that they had paid in fares for the good reason that he had their signatures to a contract for January 25th or thereabouts, and warned them in their own interests that "thereabouts" was a very elastic word.

"And I'll tell you something else," he said. "If you talk to me in this way much more, I'll have you up for riot. If you want to lose a gold mine and go to jail, that's your business and not mine."

The owner was a small man—a small man who had spent his life in the new towns of the West. The passengers were mostly hulking Swedes from the lumber camps of Minnesota and Wisconsin. They longed to lay their strong hands on him for just a moment. But it was hard to lose a gold mine, and they hadn't enough money to pay for passage on another steamer. So they slouched out of the owner's presence more in sorrow than in anger. I heard afterward that the Nancy G. finally started on February 20th. Fate was so kind to her passengers that she did not sink until the return journey. They were more fortunate than two hundred of their fellows, who saw their outfits burned on the vessel which had reached Skaguay just in time to have disembarked them in safety.

To meet the demands of the migration to the interior, Dyea and Skaguay had sprung up as quickly as a house of cards. When Indian Charlie found his nugget there was no building at Skaguay and only a trading-store at Dyea for bartering with the Indians and furnishing any supplies to an old-time prospector which he had neglected to buy at Juneau. The two towns are situated at the heads of either of two arms of the Lynn Canal, which nature has cut through the rock as man cut that of Corinth, upon sandy deposits at the mouths of the Dyea and Skaguay Rivers, and separated by a distance of a mile in a straight line over a mountain spur or of three miles around the point of the spur by water. This spur, rising into high peaks as it reaches the summit of the main range, is a barrier separating the two rivers and the two passes.

Dyea is the gateway to Chilcoot Pass, which leads to Lake Linderman, and Skaguay is the gateway to the White Pass, which leads to Lake Bennett. They were not, as it appeared to the superficial observer, trying to excel each other in wickedness, but in the amount of business that they could do. Anyone who had been a resident of either town a single day considered it his duty to warn you as a friend against the rival town and the rival pass. In a week he had become an old citizen. The small proportion who were on hand for the rush of the late summer and autumn of 1897 were as proud as Lord Mayors. Then, thousands of pack-horses, earning as high as $50 apiece a day, died from the exertions to which they were forced by their owners. In the winter their bones sticking up through the snow were snags to catch the sleds of the pilgrims. Instead of a series of steps, the packers on Chilcoot had to walk around bowlders, slipping on the fragments of crumbling rock, and possibly, after all their exertion, reaching Linderman and building their boats only to have them blocked by ice half way to Dawson, where they were effectually stranded with their outfits.

Perhaps every fifth or sixth house in the main streets was not a gambling hall or a dance hall. With these and a large idle population it is easy to understand how men who had a few dollars in cash when they arrived were obliged to sell their outfits and return home. The enforcement of law was in the hands of a United

States commissioner and three or four deputy marshals. The commissioner was a gentle optimist who spent most of his working-hours in an office with a window looking out on the river and the mountain side, where he might see no wrong-doing. "Soapy" Smith, gambler, by self-appointment, was Mayor of Skaguay and General-in-chief of the Army of Disorder, composed of characters from San Francisco and Seattle, who had no money left after their fare to Alaska was paid and were looking for something to turn up. When an atrocious murder was committed by one of his followers, "Soapy" told a body of protesting citizens that they would better mind their own business. As his army outnumbered theirs and was better armed, they accepted his advice. The United States sent out two companies of infantry, with instructions from the authorities at Washington that they should not interfere with the affairs of the two towns unless there was a riot. The Commissioner, seeming to regard their presence as an intrusion on his rights, never asked for their assistance. No murders or highway robberies were committed within sight of his little window. In time, however, "Soapy" Smith met the death that he deserved at the hands of one of his followers, and through the efforts of the merchants and the better element the towns became more orderly.

Not every pilgrim who returned home was the victim of gamblers and other parasites. For two or three days he might stop at one of the hotels until he selected the parcels of his outfit from the piles which had been thrown indiscriminately on the shore by common carriers in haste to have done with their contracts. Then, with his tent, his stove, and a cook-book, which was the gift of a baking-powder company, his journey began in earnest. The novelty of making his first flapjacks wore off by the time he had washed his dishes the second or third time. It was not long before he came to the conclusion that the fellow whom he had chosen to share all of his sorrows and joys was lazy. He blamed his own disinclination to rise in the morning and all his little failures upon him, as some men do upon their wives. Whenever he had a chance he solaced his wounded spirits by telling a stranger that he had put up with doing all of the work of his party about as long as he could.

Partnerships formed so gayly in Seattle by men who thought that being a partner was being a playfellow, could not be expected to last long at pulling sleds through the slush and going to bed in a robe or a sleeping-bag which was cheap and inefficient, with a supper of sandwiches made of sticky flapjacks and cold bacon. As he grew more angry with his partner he grew fonder of his dog. Jim might beat his poor Newfoundland, who was too nervous to pull even if he had ever been taught how; he might put up with a poor dinner; but if Tom, who was cooking, kicked the Newfoundland for stealing the bacon off the plate or sticking his nose in the butter, it was the last straw. He demanded a division of goods on the spot. But quarrels seldom resulted in blows, because they occurred when the men were too tired to do more than join in a contest of forcible language.

It was the man who leaves the door ajar at home who went to bed without washing his dishes. The Easterner now learned that, while he might know things that the Westerner did not, the Westerner knew better than he how to take care of himself. The Westerner always cooked a warm supper, and dried his footwear before going to work in the morning; while the self-neglect of the Easterner made hundreds of doctors at Dyea and Skaguay the busiest in the world. Spinal meningitis was often the penalty of sitting down to rest when dripping with perspiration without throwing a coat over the shoulders.

Even after their goods were on the summit of the Pass and the worst of their labors were over, many pilgrims gave up the battle. One by one they were thinned out until only thirty-five thousand were ready with their boats when the ice broke in Bennett. This far I had shared their experiences and then had gone on ahead. Mine was the privilege of having been a Cheechawko and at the same time standing on the river bank as an old-timer or among old-timers, to watch the arrival of the pilgrimage in its unpainted, unique flotilla.

X

PROFITS AND LOSSES

Newspapers as Profit-Winners—Hearing about Dewey—A Drop in Eggs—Market Items—Lemons against Scurvy—The Mercury at 110 degrees—An Averted Moving Day—Industrious Scavengers—The Klondyke Itself—Aspects of Summer—Bandanna Hats and Pink Lemonade—A Restaurant Trust—The Grasshoppers and the Ants—Disillusions.

IT was only to be expected that the first boat of the season to shoot around the bend above Dawson and raise a shout which would bring all the population to the shore would be manned by a resident of Seattle with the name of his beloved town painted on a huge streamer flying from the mast. Enterprising citizens of the far West such as he owned the stores at Dyea and Skaguay, the pack-mules on the trail, the restaurant tents which had sprung up in Sheep Camp, and then, following the pilgrimage on to Linderman and Bennett, generally made money out of the Klondyke without having to use a spade, because of their knowledge of the life and necessities of new communities. This proud Seattleite with the boat had two hundred dozen of nominally "fresh" eggs to sell, for which he received $3,600 within less than an hour after he had landed. Those of the crowd who could afford it hurried off to the restaurant for a "squar'" composed entirely of "ham and". The others, having to bide their time until luxuries were cheaper, found compensation in the items of news which were passed from tongue to tongue —for it had not occurred to the Seattleite to bring a newspaper with him.

"Thought there was more money in eggs," was his aggravating explanation. "'Sposed you fellers wanted to eat, not read."

As he had heard it, within a week after the declaration of war with Spain, the cruiser New York, Captain Evans in command, had reduced the fortifications of Havana in three hours. The second Cheechawko to arrive assured us that this was quite untrue, and that two of Admiral Sampson's squadron had been sunk and the Spaniards were winning on every hand. The crowd refused to believe anything of the kind, and the second Cheechawko received only $14 a dozen for his eggs.

Bargaining for a Newly Arrived Boat-Load, Dawson.

PROFITS AND LOSSES

With the next boat came a single newspaper, soiled with bacon grease. A curbstone speculator bought it for $15, stuffed it instantly into his inside coat pocket, and a few minutes later was posting signs to the effect that all might hear the news of Admiral Dewey's victory read by paying a dollar a piece that evening. His entertainment would have netted him twice as much as it did if more than three hundred and fifty people could have been packed in the hall in which it was held. Some of the wealthy men considered this proceeding an outrage on personal liberty and made it a point to buy between them any single copy of a paper later than any others that had arrived and have it read at once in the streets.

Never did contrast better illustrate the comparative reliability of even the most unreliable of modern newspapers. All winter the camp had not had so much as a small hand printing-press, and news was carried solely by word of mouth. Most miners have the weakness of exaggeration. With some it is unconscious. Others enjoy testing a hearer's credulity. Twice, up the creeks, I heard that the Continent had declared war against England and the United States; in the second instance, the de-tail of an Anglo-American naval victory off the coast of Bohemia perhaps was supplied. Such rumors were the natural fruit of the desire of Americans and Englishmen to pay compliments to one another at a juncture when the Anglo-Saxon alliance of the Klondyke was quite ready, without any assistance from London or Washington, to stand in arms against the whole world.

Within a week some thirty boats all bringing merchandise had arrived. In momentary anxiety of being lodged on a sandbar, without stopping to make camps, their crews bending to the oars night and day, they had raced with one another to the goal of high prices. Too many had placed their speculative trust in eggs. After all, there were only four hundred working claims, and the stomachs of each of their owners, and of the chief gamblers and business men, were little if any larger than that of the average human being. Eggs fell in five days from $18 to $4 a dozen and finally to $3.

A stock of fine millinery and ladies' apparel, sold to the women of the town, gave to one fellow a profit of $5,000. The first condensed milk to arrive brought $1 a can; the first butter, $2.50 a pound; the first ham,

$1.25 a pound, and the first sugar, $1.50 a pound. Lemons were more in demand in a scurvy-ridden country than oranges and bananas and sold for double their price, which was seventy-five cents apiece. But the happiest of all the newcomers was the one who had the only boat-load of boots for a community which was miserable in moccasins in warm weather. He received $15 a pair for fifteen hundred pairs which had cost him $1.75 a pair in Montreal. A five-cent bottle of ink cost $1; a fifteen-cent golf cap, $2.50; a pen-holder, fifty cents—the smallest amount of dust that anyone cared to weigh out; socks $2 a pair; a broad-brimmed summer hat, $20 to $40; a small whisk broom, $2.50; a ready-made suit of clothes, from $50 to $200; canned roast beef, $2.50 a can; canned oysters, a great luxury, $5 for a pound or pint can, and cigars, fifty cents to $1 apiece.

Against the profits which such prices represented the speculator had to set the original cost of the articles, the expense of transporting them to Dyea or Skaguay and over the one hundred and seventy-five miles to the foot of Lake Le Barge, his own fare on a steamer out of the country, and the loss of from three to six months' time.

IN THE KLONDYKE

During the lull between the arrivals of the few speculators from Le Barge and the main body of the pilgrims from Linderman and Bennett, it seemed at one time not unlikely that Dawson might be carried down the river and a new town established on some sandbar. But there was not enough snow left on the mountain sides to allow the tropical sun, shining eighteen hours out of the twenty-four and raising the mercury to 110 degrees, to accomplish its apparent purpose. Never had the old-timers known it to be so warm so early in May, and never had they known the river to be so high. They held that the Lord was displeased with the prospective defilement of the country by an army of "clerks, farmers, and dudes." The Indians knew better. White man might be very cunning in making a boat go up stream by burning wood in an iron box, but Indian could tell him some things besides how to kill moose. Old Indian could count off on his fingers some twenty years ago when the canoeing was good on the whole town-site of Dawson. That was why Indian never lived in Dawson but at Klondyke City.

Day by day we saw the water approaching a few inches nearer to our door-sill. It began to fall just as we were thinking of putting up our tent on the mountain side. Only the roofs of some cabins in Dawson were above the level of the stream. The suspension bridge between Dawson and Klondyke City, whose woven wire cables were earning two or three hundred fifty-cent tolls a day for their owners, was carried away along with a great pile of débris that it had collected. You paid fifty cents for being ferried from one island to another in the main street. Along the bank, standing in their boats, pike poles in hand, were those easy-going ones of the inhabitants who raised husky dogs for sale, did a little freighting in the winter, and took naturally to odd jobs—and I might say to squaw wives—now, in the heyday of importance, as they rowed out in the strong current and brought in a tree which had been uprooted by the flood. If the tree was suitable only for firewood it was probably worth a quarter of an ounce, or four dollars; if large enough for sawing, half an ounce. The average Klondyker's dislike for such work being quite as strong as that of the average man at home for scavenging, the easy-going had a free field and earned enough in a few days to buy winter outfits for themselves and their families. A few had even better luck. They caught portions of rafts—in two instances whole rafts—which had slipped their moorings up the river, and steering the sum of two or three months' labor of men probably unknown to them up to the bank, let the owners of the saw-mill have it at a bargain.

A source of amusement if not of income was a ditch in one of the back streets, hidden under three or four inches of water. As you stepped into it up to your thighs you heard a roar of laughter from several men sitting on a prominence near by.

"If you don't tell your friends, pardner," said one of them, "there's room up here for another, and you can enjoy yourself watchin' the others tumble in."

With all the snow gone and no rainfall, the Yukon fell as rapidly as it had risen. The thawing and crumbling soft earth of the embankments of the upper reaches made it muddier than the Missouri at its worst. For drinking water one had either to resort to the rivulets on the hill-side, amber-colored from the moss, or go to the Klondyke, which, once sluicing was nearly finished, became so clear that the bottom was visible at a depth of ten

In the Camps of the Cheechawkos.

or twelve feet, while the eddies and rapids of its current as seen from the mountain tops, left a dark, comet-like streak, stretching from its mouth for a distance of two or three miles on the café-au-lait surface of the mother stream.

By the fifteenth of June the river-bank was lined with the boats of the pilgrims, two or three deep. A city of canvas, with the old cabins and buildings as its heart, extended until the neighboring heights were dotted with tents. Knowledge of boat-building had turned out to be a misfortune, if anything, for the scows moved just as fast with the current and proved quite as easy to manage, I was told, as smaller craft pointed at both ends. The bow of each vessel bore the number which had been put on by the Mounted Police when they examined outfits for a second time for custom purposes at Le Barge or Tagish. Beside it was the name of the pilgrim's home town, of his sweetheart, his wife, or his daughter, put on with coal if he had no paint. From the mast fluttered a red bandanna, a towel, or possibly some absurdly elaborate flag which had been made in the idle hour between the completion of the boat and his embarkation. If there were three in a boat, which is the best working number for a Klondyke party, one was in the bow on the watchout for sandbars, the second was at the oars, and the third in the stern with a sweep. Navigation had its perils, too. The river as well as the Pass had claimed its victims. You heard on every hand tales of wrecks in White Horse Rapids and in Thirty Mile River, whose hidden rocks had proven even more dangerous than the White Horse Rapids. Many a scow with merchandise which had cost its owner his last cent was split in two, and those on board were thankful to find themselves on shore alive.

In their camps, the pilgrims found the mosquitoes of summer worse than the cold of winter. Fevers and headaches upon their arrival in Dawson were the consequences of exposure under the sun. It was even the fate of a few to be taken at once to the big log hospital on the hill-side which already had more patients than it could accommodate; and of a part of these to be buried in the little cemetery beyond the hospital, which gives to relatives of the deceased the sombre satisfaction of knowing that its inmates, lying at a depth where the earth never thaws, are preserved for all time—unless the town-site itself one day is marked by hydraulics.

Between the pilgrims when I met them in Seattle and when I met them again in Dawson there was all the difference of volunteers in new uniforms going forth to war and the dust-stained men who return. Their tents, so white and new in Dyea, had patches where holes had been burned by sparks or by carelessly hung candles. Their canvas bags of provender were the color of the Yukon. Their cheap sheet-iron stoves were so badly warped that the oven had ceased to bake well. Their beards were unkempt, their faces tanned. The knees of their trousers proved again how helpless a man is when alone with a needle. Many were still wearing caps. A few had made substitutes for summer hats out of wire, straw, fir twigs, and a bandanna. If the Seattle and the Vancouver merchants could have seen the outfits which they had sold after three or four months' usage, they themselves might have wondered at the skill of the manufacturers in making little seem a great deal by the use of varnish.

Very wisely the Canadian Government had provided that every pilgrim entering Canadian territory must have eleven hundred pounds, or a year's supply of food. Flour was the cheapest thing to bring an outfit that lacked two or three hundred pounds up to the requirements. Almost without exception the pilgrims had failed to realize the importance of luxuries in contributing a healthful and sustaining diet in the North. Flour sold on July 1st, after the commercial companies began to receive supplies, for $6 a sack, but white sugar sold for fifty cents a pound. Everybody had enough of staples, but many had eaten all their sugar-the larger part of their dried fruits, soup preparations, and canned delicacies and smoked or chewed all of their tobacco. It was easy to promise themselves on the trail that if they indulged themselves in "something good" after a hard day's work they could buy more of the same article in Dawson. For they were certain that a great many of their comrades intended to sell their outfits and leave the country at once—so many of their comrades did. But they, too, had eaten all their butter and evaporated eggs and kept any tobacco they had lest they should run out of it on the way home.

Pilgrims who had goods to sell hastened to

find a niche for a booth on the busy main street, where you could buy peanuts and pink lemonade, or the substantials of eating; patent leather shoes, yellow-backed novels, and cheap jewelry, or the substantials of wearing apparel. The six restaurants formed a trust and kept the price of a meal up to $2.50. In furnishing them with meat, the men who had used oxen for drawing their outfits up to the Scales and again to draw them over the lakes, now had reason to laugh back at the friends who had scoffed at them for thinking that any animal except a dog or a mule was useful in Alaska. An ox sold for $700 or $800 and was butchered at once before it had a chance to eat any more hay—which was worth $100 a ton—while the rich men stood by to see that they got the tenderloin. Besides beefsteak, we had moosesteak. One moose, who had possibly come back to his old pastures out of curiosity, was shot with a revolver only a mile out of town. His slayer, who met him ambling along the white man's trail as if he were on a stampede to some new creek, sold his carcass for $500.

Carpenters got employment at $15 a day on some one of the new dance halls, saloons, and stores which were being built as fast as green lumber for their construction could be obtained. Pilgrims without any trade, if they were wise, immediately secured logs and built a cabin, which served them at once as a temporary home, a storehouse for their supplies, and assured them warmth and shelter when winter should come. But the grasshoppers were far more numerous than the ants. The debilitating climate of summer, joined with the indecision of whether to leave the country or to remain, of whether to go down the river to the American side or up the river to Stewart if they did remain, supplied the majority with a good excuse for idleness. Some did not even put up tents on the shore, but kept house in their boats which they had moored to the bank. They sat on logs discussing their experiences in shooting the rapids, and they kept watch of the new arrivals for the purpose of guying anyone who had started before themselves but had arrived later.

There was something pitiful as well as ridiculous in the disappointment of the pilgrim who had believed everything that he read in the press-agents' pamphlets, to find that a rich claim was not to be had for working it. When he put his new gold-pan and a pack on his back and went up the trail to the creeks, where possibly he found a few colors in a rivulet, the old-timers laughed at him and asked him if he liked prospecting well enough to pan ground that was staked two years ago. If he carried a revolver they begged him, please not to shoot them. Wearily, and with all his visions dispelled, he returned to Dawson. His tent was no protection from the sun of midday. At night the light made it difficult for him to sleep. As he fried his fat bacon he could not help thinking that it was just strawberry time on the "outside."

Few pilgrims had any money and those who had were inclined to spend it on the luxuries which their palates craved. They walked up and down the main street like the crowd at a country fair; looked on at the drinking and gambling of the successful miners and marvelled at the amount of dust that passed over the saloon-keeper's scales; and slouched in and out of the stores of the two commercial companies to see the bulletin board, which had the list of names of men for whom letters had been received. If they might not visit the new variety theatre, with gambling hall and bar attached, where actresses from 'Frisco and

Seattle sang the songs of a local poet containing spirited references to the rich claim-owners —who, in return for the compliment, opened champagne at $30 a bottle between the "turns," —they could at least enjoy the sights of the river bank. In the absence of so great an event as the arrival of a scow with mules or the latest papers on board, some "pardners" were either quarrelling or dividing their outfits preparatory to selling them. With the first steamer from down the river came the news from Circle City, which meant a great deal to the old-timers. The Cheechawkos could not understand it, but, as became a crowd which gets only a glimpse into the inside world, they made the most of the peeps and simulated intense interest.

One day a midget of a steamer, the first to shoot White Horse Rapids — her parts had been packed over the Pass and put together on Bennett—ran in between two scows and tied up so quietly that not more than three or four hundred men saw it. Their pride was no greater than the disappointment of the multitude, who refused to forgive the captain until they learned that his whistle was out of gear.

Next to knowing them personally, the Cheechawkos enjoyed having the leading citizens and the foremost gamblers pointed out to them. They knew the story of how the Eldorado kings had made their fortunes, and how Jack Smith had once bet $7,000 on the turn of a card. Now and then they caught a glimpse of the tall, rawboned Scotchman who was the richest man in the country. Two years before he had been a day laborer at Circle City. When the value of Eldorado claims was an uncertain quantity he bought one of the best for $800. He spent all the first year's output in buying undeveloped properties, and then bought still others upon his promise to pay, which the miners accepted without any written word. The clean-up had vindicated his judgment. Now the fact that he had stopped on a trail to look at a claim was supposed to increase its speculative value.

And speculation still continued in both mining property and real estate. A French-Canadian who had paid $5 for a front lot just after the town-site was staked still held out persistently for $20,000, with slight prospect of getting it. The "bottom" was out of the "boom," as every man who supported himself by gambling or speculation well knew. No new strikes were made except on a few benches. None could be made on the creeks at a season of the year when the seepage from the thawing earth would fill a prospect-hole as fast as it was dug. Autumn and winter have ever been the time for prospecting in the Klondyke, and summer the time for cabin building or for taking provisions to the heads of some of the tributaries in poling-boats preparatory to prospecting.

Roughly but surely the lesson was forced home to the pilgrim that a fortune cannot be made in the Klondyke in a hurry. If he would have a claim he must find it. Even after he has found it, he must spend two or three years, unless he sells it, taking out its treasure. If it were not for the humiliation of facing their friends from whom they had parted with merry good-bys, nine out of every ten of the pilgrims would have returned home at once. Thirty per cent. of them did, as it was. Two-thirds would have gone if many had not loitered on in their tents until it was too late to go except over the ice. The tenth man developed those characteristics of patience and nonchalance in dealing with obstacles which the veteran prospector possesses by experience and by nature. For such as lacked this spirit and remained in the country there was the prospect of loitering in their cabins until their supplies were eaten, in the hope of getting a good claim on a stampede, or of going to work for wages.

In all, the pilgrims must have spent $30,000,000, or $40,000,000, on outfits and transportation. (The output of gold in the Klondyke for the year was $11,000,000.) But they have paved the way with their failures for the development of a vast expanse of country whose abounding wealth is unquestioned. The hardships of a journey to Dawson are of the past. An aërial tramway, without groans or perspiration, does the work of the packers at one-fifth of the expense on Chilcoot, and a railroad carries passengers as well as freight over the whole Pass. Steamers ply on both the upper and lower branches of the river connecting at White Horse Rapids with others plying on the lakes. Hereafter, the mines of the Klondyke will be an established institution, like the mines of California, and the prospectors who go there, better fitted for their tasks.

XI

GOVERNMENT

THE CANADIAN POLICY IN THE YUKON PROVINCE—TAXES AND FEES—THE GOLD COMMISSIONER'S OFFICE—CONFLICTS BETWEEN TERRITORIAL AND DOMINION GOVERNMENTS—TIMBER GRANTS—THE VALUE OF THE MOUNTED POLICE—THE NEWLY RICH AT DAWSON—THE ORDER OF THE YUKON PIONEERS—MRS. CONSTANTINE.

IN its policy the Dominion Government, which took matters out of the hands of the Territorial Government after the Klondyke "boom" began, has apparently been largely influenced by the predominance of aliens in the Klondyke. At least three-fourths of the 2,000 men in and around Dawson in the winter of 1897–98 and of the 35,000 pilgrims of the spring of 1898, were citizens of the United States. Naturally, the members of the Canadian Parliament regarded with dismay the prospect that the new-found wealth of a portion of their domain hitherto considered valueless was going to American mints, and that their constituents would be paying

GOVERNMENT

the expenses of administration, which, owing to the isolation of the region to be governed, must be comparatively expensive, for the benefit of another country.

Accordingly, the placer regions of the Yukon Valley lying in British territory were created a special province called the Yukon District, under the jurisdiction of the Dominion Parliament. A Commissioner, with the powers of a dictator, was appointed for the District, the Judge of the district alone being responsible to Ottawa and not subject to the Commissioner's orders. The other civil officials were a Gold Commissioner, who had charge of the recording of claims, a Crown Attorney, and two Mining Inspectors for collecting the royalties. The opportunities of the officials for their own aggrandizement were exceptional by reason of the system of taxation devised. On the output of all claims a royalty of ten per cent. was collected. Every pilgrim had to take out a mining license at a cost of $10. For having a claim recorded a fee of $15 was charged. Every alternate claim on all new discoveries was reserved to the Crown, thus depriving the community of half the reward of enterprise. These restrictions drove a great many experienced American prospectors to the other side of the boundary line and at the same time served the inexperienced as an excuse for returning home.

Major J. M. Walsh, who was chosen Commissioner, did not go to Dawson in the autumn of 1897. His corps of civil officials preceded him while he remained behind in camp on the Lewes Lakes, with a considerable force of police, in order to escort to Dawson the United States Relief Expedition.

Among the foremost charges of maladministration made against the civil officials was the one in connection with the water front, data of which were given to me by several leading men. The Canadian law provides that the main street of a new town shall be at all points a certain distance from the bank of the river. In order not to have a crooked main street, the men who staked the town-site of Dawson agreed to follow this measurement, from the greatest indentation of the bank, in a straight line. Those who bought lots on the main street supposed that they were securing river frontage, which is invaluable. The spring of 1898 however, saw a long row of buildings whose back-doors were toward the river and which faced the original row. The officials had let the water-front to an individual for a nominal sum in the name of the Government. The sub-lessees said, with a shrug of their shoulders, that they did not care to say to whom they paid their heavy rents, and that they were satisfied as long as they were left undisturbed.

Captain Constantine, who had been transferred from the charge of the police at Forty Mile to the same position at Dawson, was an old fashioned executive. His departure in the summer of 1898 was agreeable to him as well as to the other officials, because he was alone among uncongenial company. He understood the miners; and they knew that, though gruff, he was honest and incorruptible. Even the lawless ones admitted this much; for in no community is simple integrity enforced by a strong will better appreciated than in a mining-camp. Had he been retained as administrator of the whole district, with the power to choose his own assistants, Dawson would have been a phenomenally well-governed settlement from the start, and the development of the great wealth of the region would have been less retarded. Instead of men who had spent their lives among pioneers, the Dominion Government sent, as the reward for party service, men whose experience was limited to local politics at home. With hundreds of experts to choose from in British Columbia, an ex-captain of a whaler and an ex-livery-stable-keeper were made inspectors to collect the royalty of 10 per cent. on an output of eleven millions of gold.

Considering the expense of recording a claim, the owners of claims and the prospectors had at least the right to expect from the Gold Commissioner's Office reasonable attention to duty. To have posted in a public place a detailed map of the district, with all claims and the names of their owners recorded, would have required little labor and no expense; but it would have ruined the business of the clerks in furnishing information. Considering the number of policemen with idle hands, mail received in the summer might have been sorted with dispatch and distributed at different windows under different heads. But a delay of two or three days, and the prospect of waiting in line for several hours before one could even ask if there was a letter for him, were strong incentives, to miners who wished to hurry back to their claims, to put a few dollars into an itching palm, and in return to receive immediate attention at the side-door of the Post-Office.

Unfortunately the arrival of Major Walsh in Dawson in the spring was not productive of the reforms which an oppressed population had hoped for. The acts of the officials, except that of a representative of the Northwest Territory in placing a tax of $2,000 each on saloons and gambling-halls, seemed to meet with the favor of the Commissioner. He maintained that the Territorial Government was infringing on the special powers granted to him by the Dominion Government; and he issued an order that anyone who chose might sell liquor without any form of license.

The buildings on the water-front stood in the way of even a primitive system of sewerage. Simple sanitary rules were not promulgated, much less enforced. Absolutely no precautions were taken against the epidemic of fever, which was responsible for so many deaths. Private beneficence built the two hospitals, and it now maintains them and carries on all charitable undertakings. Whatever has been done in the way of improvements has been paid for by public subscriptions. The full measure of the Government's public spirit was the construction of the barracks and stockade for the Police on the Government Reserve. Had some of the money collected from the claim-owners and the prospectors been expended on constructing trails and on a system of sanitation, there would have been less ground for complaint. Doing nothing itself, the Government often took the position of the dog in the manger. The exorbitant price demanded for a charter forced capitalists to give up the plan of building a railroad from Dawson to the mines, which would have been invaluable in cheapening the cost of mining. After paying for timber privileges in their licenses, the pilgrims found, to their dismay, that the Government, or the officials, had given enormous timber grants in the neighborhood of Dawson to individuals, thus putting an artificial value on logs for firewood and building purposes.

Very properly the loudest complaints arose from Englishmen, Australians, and South Africans. If the new laws were directed against Americans, they injured Canadians and other British subjects equally as much, if not more. From the first, London regarded the Klondyke as a great field for exploration, and most of the capital represented there last spring was British.

The royalty of 10 per cent. and the failure to use the money so collected in constructing trails have been, however, more injurious to capitalistic enterprise, which is largely British, than to individual enterprise, which is largely American. A poor man who takes from $5,000 to $50,000 out of a bench-claim with his own hands will not be deterred from his labors by the royalty. But 10 per cent. on the gross output makes a majority of company propositions impracticable. Often it will wipe out a goodly profit, and put a balance on the wrong side of the ledger. As soon as it was known that the Dominion Government would not heed the appeals for the abolition of the royalty, the reaction from the "boom" was complete. The appointment of Mr. Ogilvie, the new Commissioner, who has a reputation for probity, was as welcome to the aliens as to the other residents. He at once set about the work of making reforms.

Too much cannot be said in praise of the personnel of the Northwest Mounted Police—mounted only in name, for they have not a single horse in the Klondyke—which is largely drawn from the ranks of the young Englishmen who enjoy "roughing it." In preserving order they are good-natured but severe. Malefactors are punished with the commendable promptness of British justice; and no murderer in Dawson can snap his fingers in the face of the law as one did at Skaguay. At Skaguay there was no order; at Dawson too much civil government.

For the first winter, being populated entirely by men from the old camps, Dawson was, of course, largely a sociological counterpart of Forty Mile and Circle City, except that the excitement and the feverish optimism, which increased as the new discoveries continued to surpass expectations, had hitherto been unknown in the valley. The contamination of the old customs began with the arrival of the fifteen hundred madly hastening pilgrims who succeeded in reaching Dawson before navigation was closed in the autumn of 1897. It was complete with the arrival of the great pilgrimage with its element of toughs, gamblers, and other parasites. The time had passed when every man nodded to whomsoever he met. Dawson had become a settlement not of neighbors, but, like Mecca, of strangers. The old-timers were developing those human weaknesses which are brought out in sharp relief by the sometimes doubtful blessing of great and

The Main Street of Dawson.

unexpected success. Practical communism was easier for a man when he and his comrade were equally poor than after chance had made him the owner of a plot of creek bed worth from $500,000 to $1,000,000, while his comrade, who had been too late in the stampede to stake a claim on Eldorado, was among his employees.

There sprang up as a consequence an aristocratic social circle called the Eldorado Kings, suffering, in a measure, from the affliction of the *nouveaux riches* of old communities who live miserably under the suspicion that whoever approaches them has an axe to grind. Yet they did not forget their duties to their less fortunate fellows. They gave bountifully to the churches, to the hospitals, and for the care of those poor Cheechawkos who lay ill in their tents. Upon a special occasion, the Order of the Yukon Pioneers—perhaps the death of a comrade or perhaps a church sociable, where you bought ice-cream made from condensed milk for $2.50 a plate—appeared together wearing broad blue ribands. Foremost among them was Jack McQuestion. He was keeping a trading post when the first prospectors entered the Yukon Valley. The old miners came to him to settle disputes, and the poorest of them asked him for the loan of an ounce of dust.

On the day before the departure of our steamer for the outside, attired in their best clothes and wearing their ribands, the old-timers presented to Captain Constantine an address of appreciation and a peck of nuggets. Then Jack McQuestion went over to the barracks and asked that Mrs. Constantine should share with her husband the central position in a photographic group of all the pioneers. She consented.

The Captain's wife had been her husband's companion during his service on the Yukon. When she was quite ill one winter and had to remain in her cabin from one short day's end to another—with long, dark, monotonous nights between them—the kindnesses shown to her were not limited to the devotion of her stalwart husband or the attention of ruddy-faced privates, whose Cockney accent told how far they were from the motherland of commonplaces and restraints. The miners who came to the door to inquire how she was getting on, devised means of entertaining her over their pipes and cabin fires, and then were sometimes too bashful to put them into execution.

GOVERNMENT

For one thing they learned by heart the contents of some old humorous journals in camp. Though she had been the first person to receive the journals when they had been brought down the river the preceding summer, she did not say so, and listened with gentle patience to their jokes being retold again and again.

"Mrs. Constantine," said one old-timer, as he bade her good-by, "we ain't much on manners, but we do know a lady when we see one."

XII

DOWN THE YUKON AND HOME.

GOOD-BY TO DAWSON—THE EXTINCTION OF THE UNFIT—STEAMBOATING TO ST. MICHAELS—MOSQUITOES AND SANDBARS—PILGRIMS BY THE ALL-WATER ROUTE—BEHRING SEA—CIVILIZATION ONCE MORE.

DESPITE the diet, the isolation, and the inhospitable nature of the country, many of the old-timers who had now realized the material ambition which had brought them to Alaska and were going home, saw the great crowd which gathered on the river bank to bid our steamer a pleasant voyage, disappear in the distance with a feeling of regret amounting to more than a momentary pang. From two to ten years had passed since many of them had seen a paved street.

"You'll wish you're back," and, "You won't feel natcheral," their departing friends called out to them.

Out of deference to civilization everyone had bought certain of its habiliments. New red ties stood out on the background of black sweaters, and crumpled overalls drooped over patent leather shoes. Some had taken whatever they could find to fit them, regardless of cost and incongruity. Others had halted half way in making out a wardrobe because they feared that they might not be getting the right styles or because they got indignant at the prices charged by the Dawson speculators compared with those on the outside.

The dying woman who was the mother of the first white baby born in Dawson, the sallow men who had limped down from the hospital just before the steamer sailed, and the Cheechawkos who had sold their outfits for just enough to pay for passage to Seattle, where they would have to telegraph home for railway fare—these had no regrets. We buried the woman half way down the river, two of the men before we reached St. Michaels, and a third at sea when only two days from Seattle.

With good accommodations, the journey of eighteen hundred miles from Dawson to St. Michaels would have been a pleasure trip. It was far from that with us, owing to the Spanish-American war and certain other reasons.

IN THE KLONDYKE

The commercial company which charged us $300 for transportation had two steamers at Dawson. It held them there long enough to give us the questionable satisfaction of seeing the steamer of the rival company, which had been delayed in coming up the river from its winter quarters, arrive and cut prices before our steamer, having room for seventy-five passengers, and one hundred and seventy-five on board, started on ahead of her sister steamer. We were to act as a reconnoitering force or a buffer, or whatever you choose, for the sister steamer, which had a dozen lonely, armed passengers and $2,500,000 in dust on board, with a view to saving her treasure from a Spanish privateer if one were waiting for us at the mouth of the river, as rumor from the outside said. Therefore, one hundred passengers had to sleep on the floor of the dining-room or on the lower deck among the Indians and the piles of firewood.

Except when we ate, and when the steamer poked its bow into the sand in front of some piles of fire-wood on the bank, we could be fairly comfortable lounging on the decks. For the eleven days which the journey occupied, we had one tablecloth for three sittings at each

A Dawson Good-by.

meal. As the miners had a general disregard for the utility of dishes for holding things, the cloth did not preserve its original color, even in spots, for more than two days. Our food was bad rice, bad bacon and bread, and old canned roast beef, which, however, did not count, as we could not eat it. If the company had only allowed us to use our fingers instead of forks and knives which men who were "working their fare" out as waiters washed indifferently, I should have been much happier. By July, moreover, the little mosquitoes were out. They, and not the big ones which come early in the season, understand flying straight to the mark with rigid lance. They bit the Indians as well as the white men, but to no purpose so far as making them hurry in bringing on the wood. As soon as the steamer was in midstream, the buzzing mists, which could be resisted only by the finest netting drawn over the head, disappeared.

Our principal stops in the eighteen hundred miles were at Forty Mile and Circle City, where the deserted cabins were being once more occupied and there was a chance that the old claims, which were good for their day, would be worked again, and of a recrudescence of the boom; and at Minook, where important discoveries had been made in the past winter. But we stopped also at every little Indian village—to please the Indians, one presumed—where the inhabitants came out to meet us in their light canoes and wanted to sell furs and trinkets. At many of these villages there were mission houses. We had on board a Russian priest, who had come up on the steamer from Anvik and was now returning. He was bold enough to say that he thought he needed this little recreation after having been two years alone among the Indians.

We had left behind the great mountains below Dawson, we had seen the midnight sun across the vast stretches of flats below Circle City, and were just congratulating ourselves that our Indian pilot had led us through the last of the many shallow channels in the flats, when we ran on a sandbar. Our mate and his Indian crew labored for twenty-four hours before we were off. The next day a hog chain broke and our engines were helpless. For the rest of the distance to St. Michaels we were towed by the steamer which carried the treasure and had the misery of seeing the fellows who had started two days after us and paid less fare pass us on the steamer of the rival company.

At St. Michaels we met three or four thousand pilgrims who were going into the Klondyke by the all-water route. They had bought transportation for themselves and outfits of new companies which had attempted to tow flotillas of river steamers built in Seattle to St. Michaels. Almost invariably the river steamers had been lost at sea between Seattle and Unalaska, and those who depended upon them for transportation to Dawson were only better off than others who had attempted the journey on decrepit sailing vessels that had gone to the bottom. It was a little unkind of our passengers, while we waited for transfer to an ocean steamer, to enjoy setting before them in the bluntest phrase an exaggerated account of the desperate condition of all the newcomers in Dawson.

Behring Sea was placid as a lake when we crossed it. After two days for coaling at Unalaska and after five days on the Pacific, we entered Puget Sound on the morning of July 19th. Every one on board was thinking of the steaks and the fruit that he would eat that evening for dinner. The old-timers, who had heretofore resented the steward's requests that they should not expectorate on the decks, were a little ill at ease at the prospect of the social restraint of civilization. Civilization offers many advantages over Dawson or Circle City for spending a fortune, to be sure, but such of the old-timers as were destined to become poor again—and the majority were, I think—would no doubt return to the pick and the pan as a wanderer returns home.

THE END.

BOOKS ON OUR NEW POSSESSIONS

COMMERCIAL CUBA

A Book for Business Men

By WILLIAM J. CLARK

With 8 maps, 7 plans of cities, and 40 full-page illustrations, and a Commercial Directory of Cuba. Large 8vo, $4.00

"A THOROUGHLY good and useful book. We should not know where to find within another pair of covers so much and so carefully sifted information bearing on this subject. Mr. Clark's painstaking account of the railway and telegraph systems; of highways and harbors; of rivers and water supplies, and lighthouses; of sugar and tobacco growing; and his detailed description of each province and of every city of any size, together with a 'business directory' for the whole island, make his book one of great value for reference as well as for practical guidance. In the present situation of Cuban affairs it should command a wide sale. Its accuracy is certainly of a high order."—New York *Evening Post*.

YESTERDAYS IN THE PHILIPPINES

By JOSEPH EARLE STEVENS

With 32 full-page illustrations from photographs by the author. *Seventh thousand*. 12mo, $1.50

"WITH the observant and indulgent eye of an old traveller, Mr. Stevens has seen everything in the islands worth seeing, and has described what he has seen in a most interesting manner. . . . All is set forth by the narrator in a breezy, chatty way that would be entertaining under any circumstances."
—Philadelphia *Evening Telegraph*.

CHARLES SCRIBNER'S SONS, NEW YORK

THE WAR ON SEA AND LAND

THE CUBAN AND PORTO RICAN CAMPAIGNS

By RICHARD HARDING DAVIS

With 117 illustrations from photographs and with 4 maps. *Twentieth thousand.* 12mo, $1.50

"NEVER has a war been reported as this has been, and never has a history been written like this, by one who saw it all—while the blood was hot and the memory vivid."—New York *World*.

"THIS is much the most vivid and readable of all the books on the war that have appeared so far, and it is full of life and color and incidents that show the sort of stuff of which our soldiers were made. The book is written with a keenness, a vivacity, a skill and a power to thrill and to leave an impression which mark a decided advance over anything that even Mr. Davis has written heretofore."—Boston *Herald*.

OUR NAVY IN THE WAR WITH SPAIN

By JOHN R. SPEARS

Author of "The History of Our Navy"

With 125 illustrations from photographs and with charts and diagrams. 12mo, $2.00

"MR. SPEARS has plainly put his best efforts into that mighty combat, the sea-Gettysburg of the war, the death-grapple of Cervera's ships and Sampson's. His story of the action of July 3d is superb. It is the most lucid and comprehensive description which has yet been laid before the American people, and it is made all the more valuable by the official chart of the ships' courses which accompanies it. As a whole, Mr. Spears's book is not only true to technical details, but it is a spirited and admirable piece of literary workmanship. It is one of the few volumes out of the many hurriedly issued in the wake of the war which will endure the test of time and stand as a faithful, competent picture to future generations."—Boston *Journal*.

CHARLES SCRIBNER'S SONS, NEW YORK

www.ingramcontent.com/pod-product-compliance
Lightning Source LLC
Chambersburg PA
CBHW031932230426
43672CB00010B/1902